WITH MUSTARD ON MY BACK
BY
JOHN N. MERRILL

MAPS AND PHOTOGRAPHS BY JOHN N. MERRILL

a J.N.M. PUBLICATION

1985

With Mustard on my Back
By
John N. Merrill

This book is copyright under the Berne Convention. All rights are reserved. Apart from any fair dealing for the purposes of private study, research, criticism or review, as permitted under the Copyright Act, 1956, no part of this publication may be reproduced, stored in a retrieval system, or transmitted in any other form by any means, electronic, electric, chemical, mechanical, optical, photocopying, recording or otherwise, without the prior permission of the copyright owner. Enquiries should be addressed to the publishers.

© TEXT—COPYRIGHT—JOHN N. MERRILL
© MAPS AND PHOTOGRAPHS—JOHN N. MERRILL

ISBN 0 907496 27X

The stories in the book first appeared in article form in several magazines—The Lady, Camping, Derbyshire Life & Countryside and The Great Outdoors, between 1976-1980.
FIRST PUBLISHED—SEPTEMBER 1985

J.N.M. PUBLICATIONS, WINSTER, MATLOCK, DERBYSHIRE. DE4 2DQ

CONTENTS

	Page No
INTRODUCTION	1
TWO YEARS—2,500 MILES—300 ISLANDS	3
ONE SUMMER	11
WITH MUSTARD ON MY BACK	19
PARKLAND JOURNEY	27
MY BOUNDARY WALK	39
LAND'S END TO JOHN O'GROATS	47
COASTAL REFLECTIONS	57
FOLLOW THE WHITE BLAZE	65
WALKWAY TO THE CLOUDS	71
OTHER BOOKS BY JOHN N. MERRILL	75

Yosemite Fall.

John Merrill — Resting!

ABOUT JOHN N. MERRILL

John combines the characteristics and strength of a mountain climber with the stamina, and athletic capabilities of a marathon runner. In this respect he is unique and has to his credit a whole string of remarkable long walks. He is without question the world's leading marathon walker.

Over the last ten years he has walked more than 55,000 miles and successfully completed ten walks of at least 1,000 miles or more.

His six walks in Britain are—
- Hebridean Journey .... 1,003 miles
- Northern Isles Journey .... 913 miles
- Irish Island Journey ....1,578 miles
- Parkland Journey... 2,043 miles
- Lands End to John O'Groats... 1,608 miles

and in 1978 he became the first person (permanent Guinness Book Of Records entry) to walk the entire coastline of Britain—6,824 miles in ten months.

In Europe he has walked across Austria (712 miles), hiked the Tour of Mont Blanc and GR20 in Corsica as training! In 1982 he walked across Europe—2,806 miles in 107 days—crossing seven countries, the Swiss and French Alps and the complete Pyrennean chain—the hardest and longest mountain walk in Europe.

In America he used the world's longest footpath—The Appalachian Trail (2,200 miles) as a training walk. The following year he walked from Mexico to Canada in record time—118 days for 2,700 miles.

During the summer of 1984, John set off from Virginia Beach on the Atlantic coast, and walked 4,226 miles without a rest day, across the width of America to San Francisco and the Pacific Ocean. This walk is unquestionably his greatest achievement, being, in modern history, the longest, hardest crossing of the USA in the shortest time—under six months (177 days). The direct distance is 2,800 miles.

Between major walks John is out training in his own area —the Peak District National Park. As well as walking in other areas of Britain and in Europe he has been trekking in the Himalayas four times. He lectures extensively and is author of more than sixty books.

INTRODUCTION

From the age of twelve I believed my life was to be spent in the mountains on long walks. It was to be several years before I started putting this into practice. In 1969 I went to the Island of Mull in the Hebrides and walked right round the island, about 300 miles. On the walk an idea germinated to link all the islands together in one continuous walk. I did this the following year in 1970—my first walk of 1,000 miles.

Over the next ten years (1970-1980) I walked more than 35,000 miles on major walks. I wanted to walk my own country first, and after the Hebrides walk I linked the Orkneys and Shetlands together in 1971. 1974 saw me on the west coast of Ireland walking 1,600 miles. In 1975 I did a very different walk, and walked from Norwich Cathedral to Durham Cathedral, 420 miles. In the summer of 1976 I embarked upon my longest walk so far, linking the ten National Parks of England and Wales together—a walk of 2,000 miles. The following year I was training for my British coastal walk, and walked the Pennine Way four times, 280 miles around my county boundary—Derbyshire, and a 1,600 mile Lands End—John o' Groats walk. The coast walk—6,824 miles—in 1978 was my last major walk in Britain for a while.

In 1979 I left our shores for the first time, and walked 2,100 miles on the Appalachian Trail in America, as a training walk, and in Europe the Tour of Mont Blanc (100 miles). In 1980 I walked from Mexico to Canada via the Pacific Crest Trail—2,700 miles—a truly exceptional walk, and one that I plan to do again.

In this book I have gathered together the stories of all my principal walks between 1970—1980, and included my basic schedules of the route and a detailed map. I have enjoyed doing all the walks, and plan to keep walking.

Since the walks in this book, I have been to the Himalayas four times, walked across Austria—700 miles in training— completed a 2,800 mile walk across Europe, the Alps and the Pyrenees, and in 1984 a 4,226 mile walk across the U.S.A. What next you may ask? Already planned are a 2,500 mile walk down the length of New Zealand, a 'world' walk, doing walks in four continents; a 7,000 mile walk across America from the east coast to the west; and a 4,000 mile walk from Canada to Mexico. The next decade of walking looks exciting!

Walking means a great deal to me, and I hope from my brief stories of my walks that I share something of the joys of marathon walking with you.

Happy walking.

JOHN N. MERRILL
Winster—JUNE 1985.

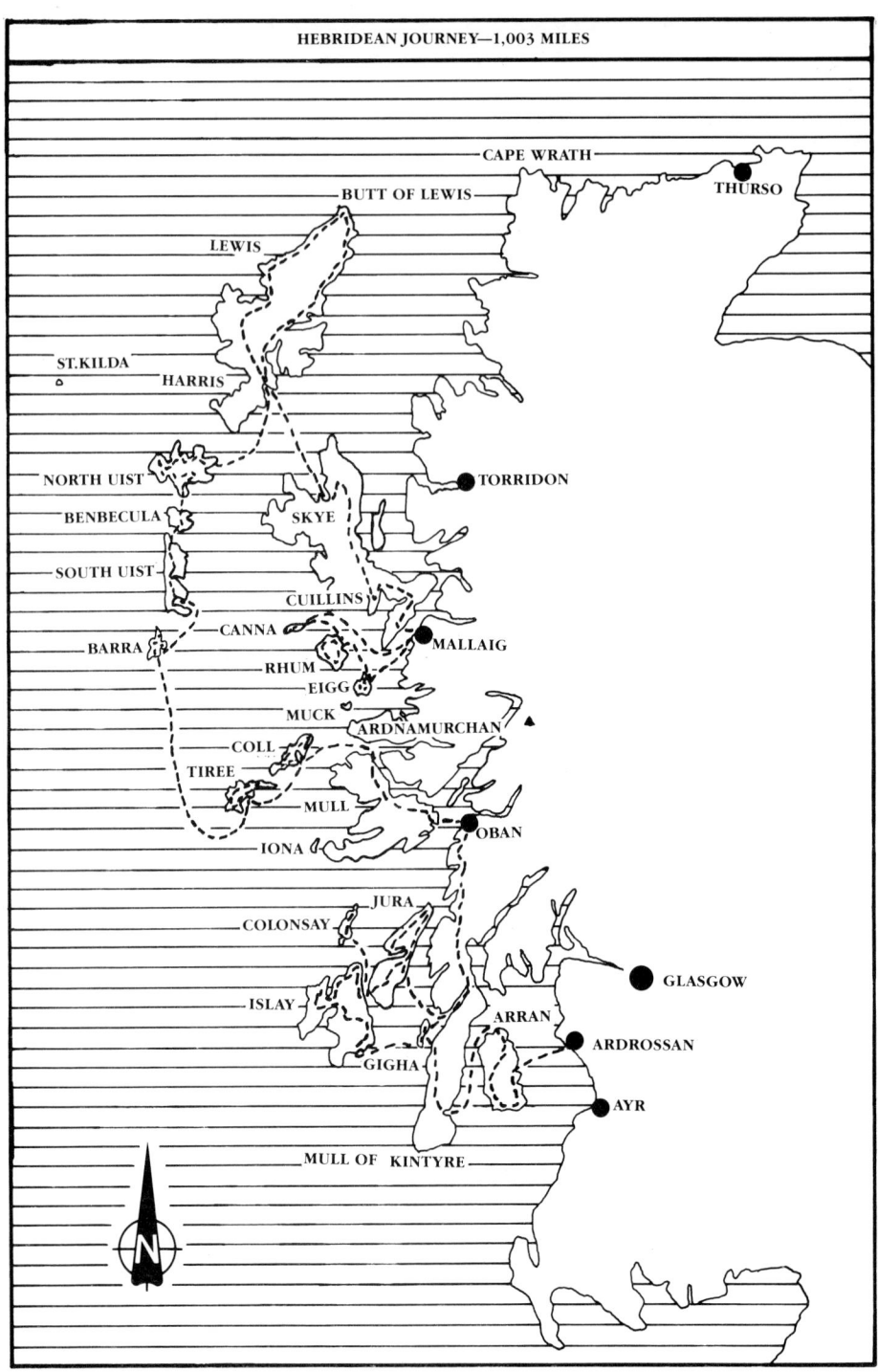

TWO YEARS—2,500 MILES—300 ISLANDS

Walking along the shore of Brodick Bay on Arran late one September, I mused at the thought of walking through all the Hebridean islands in one go. The idea gripped me completely, and in May the following year I set off; in two months I had walked over 1,000 miles and been on the majority of islands. That accomplished, my thoughts turned to the Orkneys and Shetlands, and again the following year I did a walk of over 1,000 miles through them. One island remained, whose name is sheer magic—St. Kilda. Within the two year period of setting off on my Hebridean journey, I was on that island. Looking back now on the two years, I feel extremely humble in having the good fortune and time to explore them. I am no island bagger, just a long distance walker who has a taste for the unusual and an insatiable appetite for peaceful scenery.

Carrying a 40 lb. rucksack complete with tent and bare necessities, I boarded the ferry at Ardrossan and crossed the Firth of Clyde to Arran, the first island of my Hebridean Journey. The sun shone brilliantly, and I little knew that for the next five weeks the weather would not change. Incredibly, out of 54 days on the walk, I had only three rainy days. Arran proved a good week's walk, through its mountains and gentler southern half. While waiting for the ferry for Campbeltown from Lochranza, I counted twenty-three blisters! A hard fact of long distance walking, but after a couple of weeks your feet are as hard as nails. From Campbeltown my route lay through the Kintyre Peninsula to Tayinloan for the boat to Gigha. From the southern tip of the island I picked up another boat for Port Ellen on Islay and the start of the Hebrides proper. Islay has few equals for its scenic coastline and beautiful sandy beaches. The walk up the western side of the island to Rhuuval Lighthouse was one of the finest on the whole journey—just the golden sands, oystercatchers, wild goats and red deer. Gaining Port Askaig, I viewed the Paps of Jura with respect and caught the boat to Colonsay. When the tide went out I walked across a mile of sand onto Oronsay to see the ruins of St. Oran's Chapel and the collection of stone crosses and grave slabs. Back on Colonsay I headed for the gardens of Colonsay House and the matchless Kiloran Sands.

Returning to Port Askaig, I switched boats and reached Jura. For three weeks those noble Paps had dominated the scene. I camped at their base, and the next day climbed all three—and the little Pap for devilment as I headed northwards to Tarbert. Few islands compare with the attractions of Jura with its raised beaches on the western side, its remoteness and awe-inspiring Gulf of Corrievreckan with its whirlpool. I camped overlooking the gulf before walking down the western side. At Glen Carisdale I startled a yachtsman who had rowed ashore. On catching his breath, he said, 'Ah, Dr. Livingstone, I presume.' Being deeply tanned, wearing shorts and sporting a three week beard, the description was not too inapt.

From Craighouse, Jura's capital, I caught the boat back to the mainland and began the long walk to Oban. Arriving there two days later, I could see my next island—Mull. I had used Mull as a training ground for the walk the previous year, and having walked all round it I simply walked from Craignure through the mountains to Salem and Salem Forest and on to Tobermory. Here I caught the Hebrides-bound boat, and leap-frogged to the islands of Coll, Tiree, Barra and finally to Lochboisdale on South Uist. Walking

Castlebay, Barra, Outer Hebrides.

Trotternish Ridge, North of The Storr, Isle of Skye.

to the northern tip of Coll along the lily-filled lochs of the east coast, I came to Sorisdale. A more beautiful place would be hard to find, with a thatched cottage and sandy beach.

I sat overlooking the beach and gazed at the scene. Then suddenly out of the cottage came four sheepdogs bounding towards me, followed by six cats and finally four bachelors. Minutes later I was sitting beside a peat fire and enjoying their company. During the conversation I mentioned that I would finish the walk on Canna. At this their eyes lit up. Shyly they asked if I would convey their greetings to the Post Mistress there. I said I would, and that I should reach the island in five weeks' time. They hadn't seen her for ten years!

On Barra I watched the daily plane come down on the hard shell sand of Traigh Mhor before walking to Scurrival Point and looking across the Sound to South Uist. From Lochboisdale I walked northwards through the mountains of the eastern side and visited the nature reserve at Balranald. Beyond it I came to the 27 ft. high statue of Our Lady of the Isles. A short distance later I walked across the road bridge onto Benbecula, and the following day on to North Uist. All the time the prominent shape of the mountain Eaval stood challenging. The mountain was hard to ascend, and, being surrounded by lochs, an approach to it requires careful map reading.

Entering Lochmaddy two days later, the weather broke, and for the next 36 hours there was a torrential downpour. I continued my walk as planned, and caught the boat to Tarbert on Harris. Although soaked to the skin, I crossed through the mountains to the west coast and the Callinish Stones and headed for the Butt of Lewis. Two days later I stood at the Butt with tears in my eyes. This was my furthest point northwards, and with over 700 miles on foot behind me I felt sad, but cheered up knowing that there was more than 300 miles still to walk! I headed southwards along the east coast to Stornoway, and eventually to Tarbert. In Stornoway it felt strange seeing so many people, shops and a supermarket. I stayed for an hour, but then lost my nerve and fled.

From Tarbert I caught the boat to Uig on Skye and began the long walk through the island. First I headed to the Quirang, before following the ridge all the way to the Storr. Although tired, I thought it was, and must rate as, one of the finest walks in the Hebrides. Leaving Portree behind, I crossed through the Cuillins in atrocious weather to Elgol, and then through the Sleat Peninsula to Armadale. The next day I returned to the mainland at Mallaig and purchased my last week's food for the final islands of Eigg, Rhum and Canna. I spent two days on each, tying in with the ferry times. On my final day on Canna, I did as asked and visited the Post Mistress, but alas, she could not remember the four bachelors. I left the next afternoon, knowing I had completed the walk but with a deep sadness within me.

That winter the maps were once again laid out on the table and the basic plan of a walk through the islands of the Orkneys and Shetlands was made. Being so scattered, I would not be able to do a continuous walk as in the Hebrides, but would have to have a central base as I moved nothwards. The contrast between the two island groups was deeply marked. The Orkneys having lush green gentle rolling hills, sandy beaches and rugged coastline. The Shetlands were a contrast, being high and of a more rugged nature. Both had their irresistible charm and my memory never tires of recalling the captivating scenes of shore, wildlife and people.

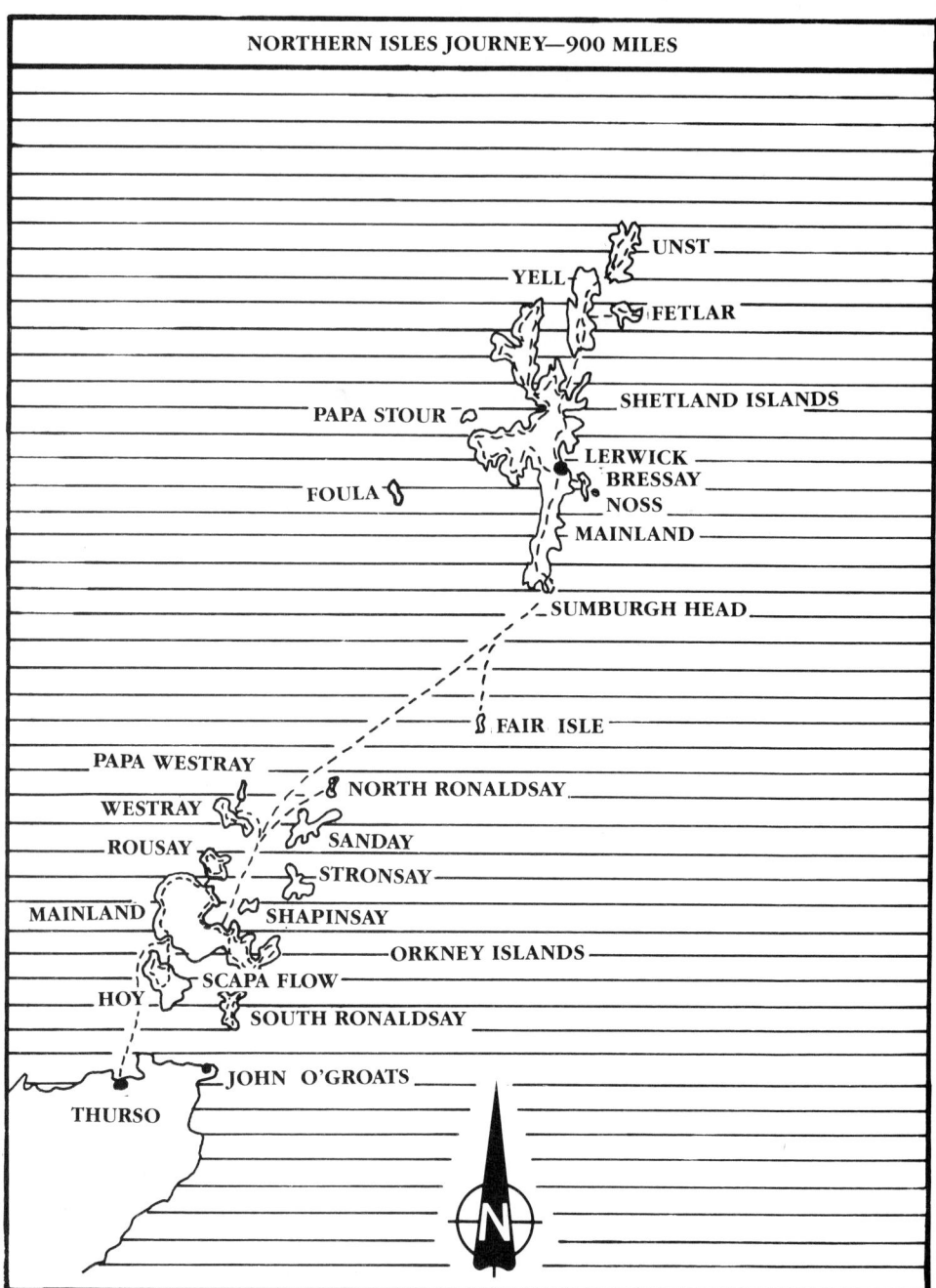

Catching the boat at Scrabster I arrived at Stromness in the Orkneys after passing the renowned Old Man of Hoy. From there I caught a boat to Hoy and camped on the beach of Rackwick Bay. Next day I had a close look at the 450 ft. high rock stack. Back on the Orkney mainland, it was around the coastline to Yesnaby and the neolithic village of Skara Brae. Further round I went onto the island of Rousay to see its brochs and amazing collection of chambered cairns. Back on the mainland once more, I headed southwards to Kirkwall and its magnificent red stoned St. Magnus Cathedral, before continuing down the eastern side over the Churchill barriers and onto South Ronaldsay. On Lamb Holm I visited the simple but beautiful Italian Chapel.

Returning to Kirkwall, I began catching the mailboats to Shapinsay, Westray, Sanday and North Ronaldsay. The latter was a remarkable island; being small, the islanders have built a wall around its perimeter to preserve the grass for their cattle and crops. The sheep are confined to the shore, and although small and thin live healthily on seaweed. After exploring Noltland Castle on Westray, I walked along a sandy beach and was attacked by a large colony of nesting terns, who took to the air and swooped down at my head. Earlier, on Hoy, I experienced the dive-bombing antics of a Great Skua as I crossed through its terrain. Like the terns, this was an alarming experience, but one I became used to as I moved northwards.

After a month's walk around the Orkney islands, I caught a plane and flew to the Shetlands, landing at Sumburgh Head. On the 25 minutes' flight I saw my next island, Fair Isle. The next day I caught the twice-weekly boat, the 'Good Shepherd', and after a rough crossing arrived at this, one of Britain's most attractive islands. For three days we had a force 9 gale blowing, which created dramatic scenes of pounding, swirling seas. The island's coastline is scattered with rock stacks of varying shapes and sizes, creating unforgettable scenes. The cliffs support a wide variety of sea birds, with kittiwakes, guillemots, razorbills and the lovable puffins. Islands grip you in their charm, but Fair Isle makes you addicted. I left with a sense of longing.

Returned to the Shetland mainland after a week on the island, I began the long walk through the mainland towards Yell and Unst. En route I visited the island of Mousa with its spectacular broch and herd of Shetland ponies. At Lerwick I camped beside the graveyard overlooking Bressay Sound, before crossing to Bressay to reach the island of Noss. This island has a large gannetry on its 600 ft. high eastern cliffs and makes fascinating observation. You watch the gannets fly in their nests, or seawards to make their alarming but perfectly controlled dive for fish. After two weeks' walk I gained Unst, and began walking towards Haroldswick, where there is the most northern post office and petrol station in the British Isles. Leaving them behind, I walked the final seven miles onto Hermness and looked out over half a mile of sea to Muckle Flagga and the Outer Skerries, the northern extremity of our archipelago. London was 900 miles away.

Walking back through Unst I caught the boat across to Yell, and at the village of Mid Yell I was fortunate enough to get a boat across to Fetlar. Apart from being home to a Snowy Owl, there are several red phalropes on the lochs. My second night there was spent attending the annual dance and sale of goods for the Church Fund. The sight will never be forgotten, as all manner of items were sold—such as a quarter pound of sweets for £1! In two hours more than £180.00 had been raised. Two days later Bobby Tullock took me back to Yell, and I continued my walk back to the mainland and onto the Point of Fethaland and the remarkable sea-torn rocks and cliffs of Eshness. A week

Old Man of Hoy, Isle of Hoy, Orkneys.

Main Street, St. Kilda.

later, after failing to get to Foula, I had completed my walk. Heavy—hearted I boarded the boat at Lerwick bound for Aberdeen. As I had been walking in both the Hebrides and Northern Isles, everyone had uttered the legendary words of St. Kilda. Back home from the Shetlands I learned how to get there. When it was time to book, I contacted the Scottish National Trust and was fortunate in securing a place in one of their working parties. Twelve people from assorted ways of life met on Oban pier, and left an hour later bound for the island. The two-week stay on St. Kilda has no equal in Britain. It is beyond doubt the ultimate in island exploration, and for me a fitting climax to my two years of island wanderings. To walk round the village bay and gaze at the jagged coastline of Dun, to walk over to Glen More and descend the tunnel, to ascend Connachair and peer down the 1,400 ft. sea cliffs or look across the sea to Boreray and Stack Armin and Lee, is to sample the sheer majesty of superlative scenery and work of nature.

Back home as I write this and reflect on the two years, I still cannot grasp my sheer good fortune at seeing so much in so short a time. The walks were hard, and often I had blistered feet and aching limbs, but I would do it again to see such beauty. Simply, thank you. I will return.

☆☆☆☆☆☆

Suggested further reading—
From Arran to Orkney John N. Merrill Holmes McDougall 1981
Island Years F.Frasher Darling Readers Union 1952
The Scottish Islands George Scott-Moncrieff Oliver & Boyd 1961
Rambles in the Hebrides Roger A. Redfern Robert Hale 1966
A Tangle of Islands L.R.Higgins Robert Hale 1971
Shetland James R. Nicolson David & Charles 1972
St Kilda and other Hebridean Outliers Francis Thompson David & Charles 1970
The Life and Death of St Kilda Tom Steel National Trust for Scotland 1965
Island on the Edge of the World Charles Maclean Tom Stacey 1972

The Gannetry on the Island of Noss, The Shetlands.

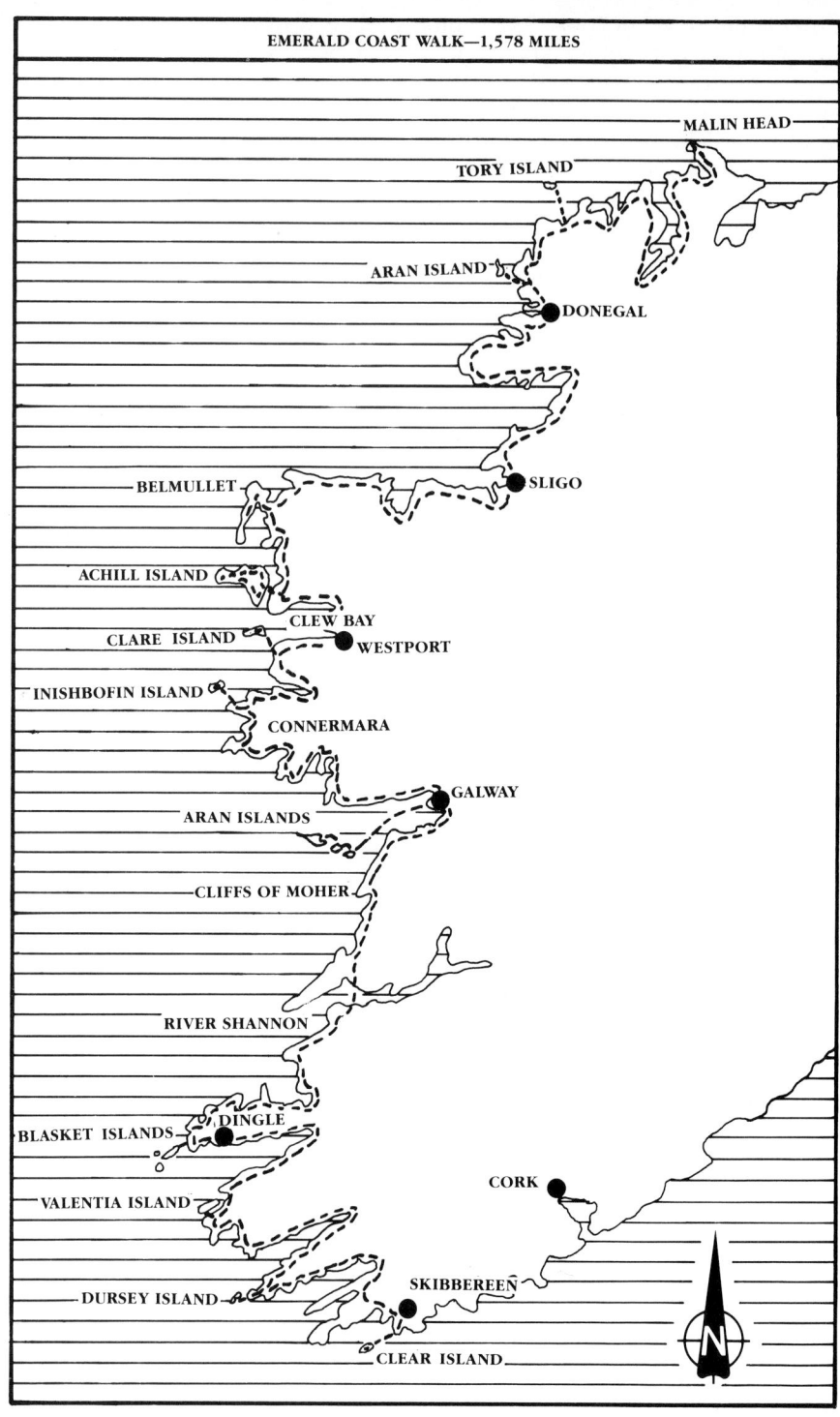

ONE SUMMER

The tower on the summit of Malin Head lay in front of me. I walked slowly but purposefully towards it, dreading the moment of arrival. With a feeling of intense sadness I stood beside it and looked down at the heaving sea as it crashed relentlessly against the rocks. For the last 78 days I had walked the whole length of the west coast of Ireland, from Cape Clear Island. A walk of just under 1,600 miles. I couldn't grasp that I had made it. I let the sea wash around my boots before heading southwards back to England. For a while I would let events take their course before I could, several months later, look back on the summer of '74 and my walk.

It was my third walk over 1,000 miles, and the completion of an island trilogy of walks—the Hebrides, the Northern Isles and now the west coast of Ireland. In many ways it was like a dream—incredible scenery, few people, sandy beaches to oneself—and I did not see another walker for three months! Cape Clear in County Cork is the most south-west point of Ireland, and was, therefore, a fitting place to begin the walk. The island is small with a population of just over 200. There are few cars, and only about 10 miles of metalled, single track roads. On my first night there I witnessed one of the most incredible sunsets I have ever seen. The sun passed through a layer of cloud, sending out shafts of golden light in all directions. The omens looked good, or so I thought. Little did I know it would rain for three weeks in June, the whole of July and much of August! But, like they say, it is 'soft' rain and one does not object to getting wet.

A week later, with the first hundred miles covered, I reached Garnish Island at the head of Bantry Bay. The island has been converted from a rocky barren surface to one covered with trees, and is full of exotic plants. Seeing it on a hot sunny afternoon at the beginning of June, when all the azaleas and rhododendrons were at their best, was a wonderful experience. The work was largely done by a Scotsman, Annan Bryce, who purchased the island in the latter half of last century and whose son completed the work this century and gave it to the Irish nation.

At the mouth of the bay I approached another fascinating island, Dursey Island. Like all islands, the population has and still is steadily declining. Today only about forty people live there. Instead of reaching the island by boat, I sat in a cable car cabin and swayed some 70 ft. above the waves as it made the 500 yard crossing. The cable car was installed in 1969, and it was hoped that it would halt the depopulation, but this has not happened. The island gives the impression of being rundown, with no tarmaced roads and no electricity, but scenically it is beautiful, with a jagged coastline and a gannetry offshore.

Ten days later, walking round the Dingle Peninsula, through Ryan's Daughter country, I came down to Dunquin and into Kruger's Bar. Here I sought out the boatman, and, when sufficiently lubricated with Guinness, I asked him to take me across to the Blasket Islands. He agreed, and said to be down at the pier at 10.30 a.m I, in my usual English promptness, arrived at 10.15 a.m., and he calmly sauntered down at midday! Three of us carried his curragh boat on our shoulders and gently placed it in the water. These traditional boats of the west coast are made of a thin wooden frame covered with canvas and tarred. Being so light, the oar has no blade, otherwise it would turn the boat over.

The Blasket Islands are the nearest parish to America, which lies 2,800 miles westwards. In 1953 the islanders left Great Blasket, the largest island, to continue their lives on the mainland. The population had declined, and the young had either emigrated to America or were working in England. Visiting the island, it was sad to see the village slowly crumbling into ruins. An abandoned jolting cart stood forlornly on the grass track, a cooking pot was half covered with thistles, and the church bell looked over the houses. Behind the village rose the island's backbone, a mountain ridge rising to a height of 900 ft The walk along it with sheer sides dipping down to the blue sea was a captivating walk. The weather was perfect, with no wind, few clouds, and a motionless sea. It is on days like these that the serenity of islands becomes most marked.

After crossing the river Shannon on the car ferry from Tarbert, in pouring rain, I approached the Cliffs of Moher in County Clare. Unknowingly, I reached the cliff top at its southern end and gazed breathless at the sight. The cliffs curved away to my right, rising in height to over 600 ft The restless sea pounded against their bases, sending spray high into the air. The ledges were bursting with sea birds—guillemots, kittiwakes, razorbills, fulmars, shags and puffins, and a pair of peregrine falcons surveyed the appetising scene from above. The cliffs stretch for four miles, and it is possibly the finest cliff walk in Ireland. At their northern end is O'Brien's Tower, which now acts as an information centre, but from whose top one can survey Galway Bay and the fabled Aran Islands.

To reach these islands I had first to cross another absorbing area, the Burren. The Burren covers an area of 100 square miles and is one huge limestone pavement. I walked across the centre, covering 27 miles. Apart from the scenic qualities of the area, the main attraction is wild flowers, for many alpine plants grow profusely here at sea level. The ground was covered with purple cranesbill, thousands of spotted heath orchids, hartstongue ferns grew out of the jointing crevices, and purple saxifrage was in abundance. Nearing the end of the plateau in the late evening, I disturbed a couple of red foxes who fled at the sight of a human.

Burren Country, Co. Clare.

The boat rode the waves well as it crossed Galway Bay bound for the Aran Islands. These three islands, Inisheer, Inishmaan and Inishmore guard the entrance to the bay and are an extension of the limestone plateau. Life on the islands is hard; being so rocky, there is little arable land, and what there is has been man-made over the years. The islands are naturally famous for the Aran knitwear, but little is made on the island today. As I walked round the islands, I saw only one woman actually knitting an Aran pullover, and as soon as I produced my camera she disappeared. Inishmore, the big island, has an impressive west coast, where the cliffs rise to 300 ft. high and overhang at the top. In olden days the islanders would fish off these overhanging rocks by passing the line between their toes. On getting a catch, they had to haul the fish up the 300 ft. The island's other major attraction is its ancient monuments, with numerous early churches and crosses, and several spectacular forts. Dun Mor, which was built 2,000 years ago, completely encircles the cliff, and with three defence walls was an exceptional stronghold. Returning to Galway, the remainder of my walk—and there was still over 800 miles to do—lay through the rugged and beautiful Connemara, then on to County Sligo and finally Donegal. Just off the northern coastline of Connemara lay Clare Island. I managed to catch the thrice-weekly mailboat to the island. Stepping ashore, I saw a notice in the Post Office window stating that postal collections were on a Monday, Wednesday, Friday and Saturday, but were variable! Minutes later, I erected the tent on a patch of grass above a sandy beach. As I was putting in the pegs I heard a donkey behind me I looked up and saw the island postman astride his donkey, and about to set off to deliver the mail to the islanders. Walking around the island I came to the grave of Grace O'Malley. She was a notorious woman of the 16th Century who ruled a large area of the west coast. The island still has her castle. Any passing boat that did not pay her toll was unmercifully blown up. On the marital side, she married four times. Each husband was especially chosen for his wealth and strategic castle. About a year after the marriage he would die mysteriously and her supporters took over his castle.

Islanders carrying a Currach, Inisheer, Aran Islands, Co. Galway.

Back on the mainland I ascended Ireland's holy mountain, Croagh Patrick, before walking around Clew Bay and seeing over 300 islets in the bay. After gaining Valencia Island, I walked through some of Ireland's most desolate scenery, where you can see no house for miles and only the featureless landscape of peat greets the eye, until the town of Belmullet. A week later I was in County Sligo, and visited Yeats' grave before seeing his favourite mountain, Benbulben. Reaching Donegal, the first pangs of regret were felt, for I knew I was on the final lap of the walk. After climbing the county's highest mountain, Errigal, I descended to the sea, and luckily caught a boat to Tory Island.

Tory Island has no equal in the British Isles and is, for me, our finest island. It is small; being only three miles long and no more than half a mile wide, and has a population of about 400. The island's main attraction is its remoteness. Even in summer you do not know when you will get out to the island, and once there you do not know when you will return. In the winter the island is quite often cut off for eight weeks at a time through bad weather. Another attraction is that modern life has not encroached on their way of life. There are no cars, just four tractors; only four telephones; no pub; and they have had electricity for only three years. In the houses, peat is still the main heating fuel. Coupled with these is an incredible west coast, which is twisted and contorted into stunning shapes, and many rock stacks lie just offshore. At the pier can be found a unique curragh boat, only found on this island. It is much smaller than the ones used on the Blasket and Aran Islands, and has no keel.

After three days of bad weather, the island's boat made the crossing to the mainland and I began the final leg of the walk—168 miles in six days. By now I was very fit, deeply suntanned and hated knowing that the end was near. I had set off in the early summer, walked through mid-summer's day and now walking in late August as the nights began to draw in and become cooler. It had been a unique and very profound experience, and one that I will cherish for the rest of my life. I would willingly do it again and see the summer pass as I walked in matchless scenery.

Boots after completing his 1,578 mile Irish walk.

IRISH ISLAND JOURNEY—1974

Major breakdown of route

Day

1	Train from Manchester to Holyhead. Boat across to Dublin. Train to Cork. Bus to Skibbereen. Skibbereen—Isle of Innishbeg.	*(4m)*
2	Isle of Innishbeg—Rinarogy Island—Baltimore—Clear Island.	*(8m)*
3	Clear Island.	*(8m)*
4	Clear Island—Baltimore—Sherkin Island.	*(8m)*
5	Sherkin Island—Schull—Mt. Gabriel—Drishane Bridge.	*(10m)*
6	Drishane Bridge—Knockboolteenagh—Bantry—Glengarriff.	*(20m)*
7	Glengarriff—Garinish Island—Caha Mountains—Knockowen—Hungry Hill—Knocknagree—Maulin—Hearhaven.	*(20m)*
8	Bearhaven—Bear Island.	*(15m)*
9	Bear Island—Bearhaven—Pulleen Harbour—Garinish—Dursey Island.	*(15m)*
10	Dursey Island—Dursey Head.	*(10m)*
11	Dursey Island—Garrish Bay—Ballydonegan Bay—Mt. Knockgour—Eagle Hill—Maulin—Tooth Mountain—Kilmakilloge Harbour.	*(20m)*
12	Kilmakilloge Harbour—Lauragh—Knockater—Ardea—Kenmare.	*(15m)*
13	Kenmare—N. coast to R. Kenmare to base of Eagles Hill.	*(19m)*
14	Eagles Hill—Mullaghbeg—Ballybrack—Ballinskelligs Bay—Ballinskelligs—Bolus Head.	*(20m)*
15	Bolus Head—St. Finan's Bay—Portmagee—Valencia Island—Reenard Point.	*(20m)*
16	Reenard Point—Skellig Islands.	
17	Reenard Point—Mt. Knocknadobar—Mt. Foley—Coomacarrea—Seefin.	*(20m)*
18	Seefin—Killorglin—Castlemain Harbour—Inch.	*(22m)*
19	Inch—Annascaul—Dingle—Ventry—Mount Eagle—Dunmore Head.	*(22m)*
20	Great Blasket Island.	
21	Dunquin—Smerwick Harbour—Brandon Mountain—Brandon Peak—Shevanea—Stradbally Mt.	*(24m)*
22	Stradbally Mt.—Knockbeg—Slieve Mish Mountains—Tralee.	*(22m)*
23	Tralee—Barrow Harbour—Banna Strand—Kerry Head—Ballingarry.	*(23m)*
24	Ballingarry—Kilmore—Moneycashen—Ahafona—Knockanmore Mt.—Astee—Bunaclugga Bay.	*(24m)*
25	Bunaclugga Bay—Ballylongford—Saleen—Tarbert—Ferry—Killimer—Kilrush.	*(16m)*
26	Kilrush—Scattery Island—Doonbeg—White Strand.	*(10m)*
27	White Strand—Kilmurry—Spanish Point—Rinneen—Liscannor Bay—Cliffs of Moher.	*(22m)*
28	Cliffs of Moher—Roadford—Slieve Elva—The Burren.	*(20m)*
29	The Burren—Gortaclare Mt.—Kinvarra—Kiloolgan—Cranmore—Galway.	*(25m)*

30	Inishmore, Aran Islands—northern half of island.	(14m)
31	Inishmore, Aran Islands—southern half of island.	(14m)
32	Inishmaan—Aran Islands.	(8m)
33	Inisheer—Aran Islands.	(8m)
34	Back to Galway—Barna—Spiddle—Inveran—Costello—Annaghvaan.	(24m)
35	Annaghvaan—Lettermore Island—Gorumna Island.	(20m)
36	Lettermore Island—Costello—Derryrush—Avogh Rock—Loch Skannive—Finish Island.	(22m)
37	Finish Island—Mweenish Island—Glinsk—Cashel—Canal Bridge—Ben Corr—Twelve Pins.	(18m)
38	The twelve Pins of Connemara—Ben Baun—Tisvebaun—Streamstown—Omey Island—Gleggan.	(20m)
39	Gleggan—mail boat for Inishbofin Island	(6m)
40	Inishbofin.	(6m)
41	Inishbofin—Myard—Letterfrack—Mt. Doughruagh.	(10m)
42	Mt. Doughruagh—Garraum—Killary Harbour—Ferry—Mweelrea Mts.—Killadoon—Roonah Quay.	(22m)
43	Roonah Quay—Mailboat to Clare Island.	(10m)
44	Clare Island—Roonah Quay—Old Head—Croagh Patrick—Westport Bay.	(14m)
45	Westport Bay—Westport—Newport—Rosturk.	(20m)
46	Rosturk—Corraum Hill—Achill Sound—Knockmore—Dooega—Trawmore Sand—Keel.	(20m)
47	Keel—Dooagh—Achill Head—Oroaghaun—Slievemore—Cashel—Achill Sound.	(22m)
48	Achill Sound—Lock Gall—Glaggan Mountain—Glennamong—Nephin Bay—Corslieve.	(20m)
49	Corslieve—Maumybelly—Knockletterness—Bangor—Glencastle Hill—Belmullet.	(20m)
50	Belmullet—Saleen Harbour—Elly Bay—Termon Hill—Garvecarrick—Cross Point—Belmullet.	(15m)
51	Belmullet—Corlogh—Erris Head—Tower Hill—Belmullet.	(15m)
52	Belmullet—Baratra—Glenamoy—Glinsk.	(20m)
53	Glinsk—Belderg—Maumabeogh—Killala.	(20m)
54	Killala—Bunree—Ox Mountains—Loch Talt.	(20m)
55	Loch Talt—Loch Easky—Ox Mountains—Collooney.	(22m)
56	Collooney—Ballysadare—Cunmeen Strand—Coney Island—Ferry to Rosses Point—Drumcliff.	(16m)
57	Drumcliff—Grange—Mullaghmore—Isle of Inishmurray.	(14m)
58	Mullaghmore—Tullaghan—Bundoran—Ballyshannon—Coolmore.	(18m)
59	Coolmore—Ballintra—Laghy—Donegal—Banagher Hill.	(18m)
60	Banagher Hill—Blue Stack Mountains—Loch Muck—Doocharry.	(20m)
61	Doocharry—Dunglow—Burtonport—Cruit Island—Burtonport.	(20m)
62	Ferry to Aran Island.	(10m)
63	Ferry from Aran Island—Burtonport—Amnagary—Bunbeg—Falcarragh.	(20m)

64	Mailboat to Tory Island.	(6m)
65	Tory Island.	(6m)
66	Tory Island.	(6m)
67	Magheroarty Pier—Falcarragh—Muckish Mountain—Loch Beagh.	(14m)
68	Loch Beagh—Loch Gartan—Gregory Hill—Letterkenny—Manorcunningham—Ballylawn.	(20m)
69	Ballylawn—Drumboy—Speenage—Inch Top—Inch.	(18m)
70	Inch—Keenkeeragh Hill—Slieve Snaght—Carndongah	(18m)
71	Carndonagh—Malin—Umgall—Ardmalin—Malin Head	(12m)
72	Malin Head—End of journey.	

Total mileage of the journey—1,178 miles (on paper)—in fact it turned out to be 1,578 miles on the ground.

Rossaveal, Connemara, Co. Galway.

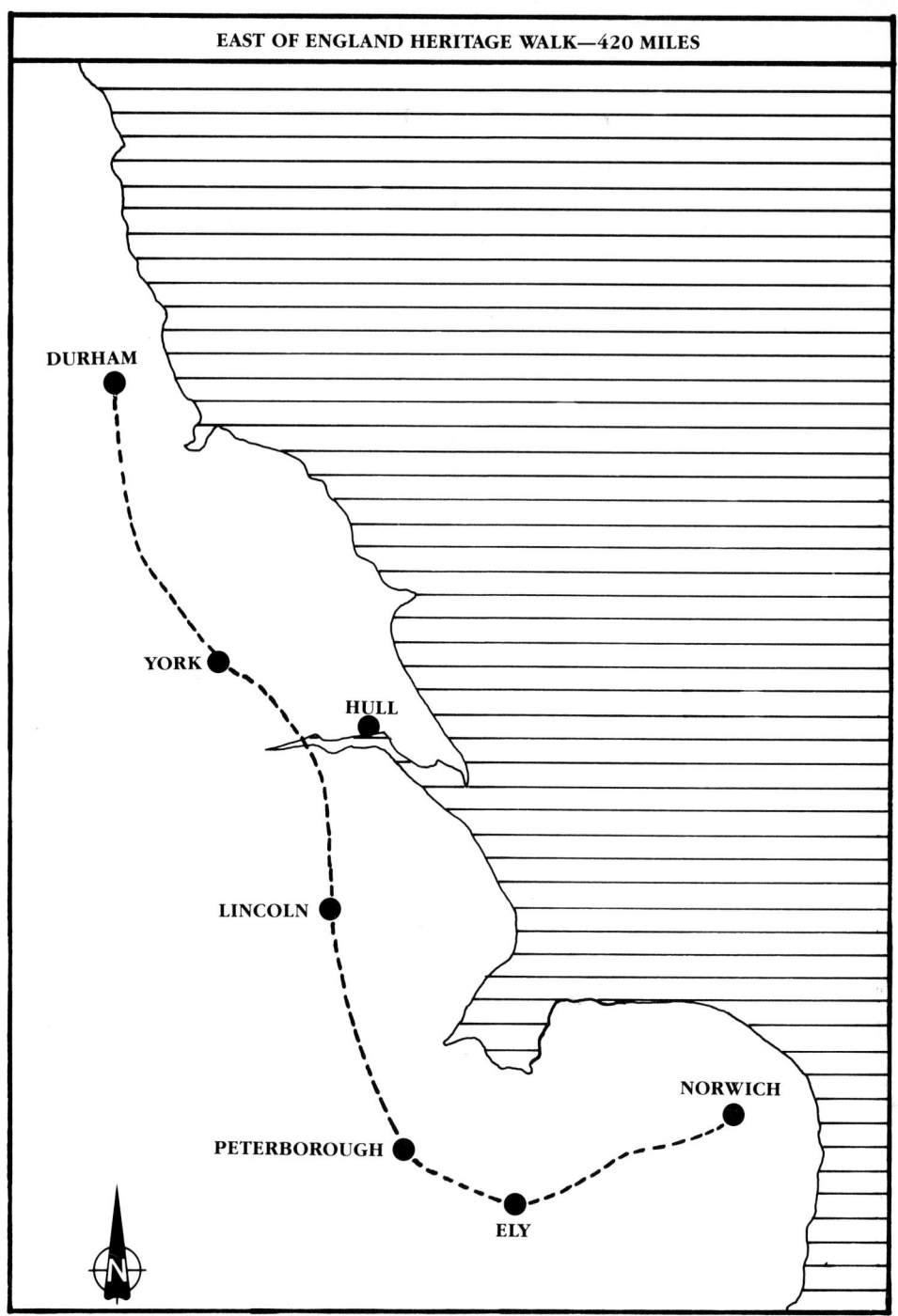

WITH MUSTARD ON MY BACK

During the early Spring of 1975, when the late winter snows descended upon us, I set off from Norwich on the 15th March to walk up the eastern side of England. My aim over the next 21 days was to walk from Norwich to the mediaeval cathedral cities of Ely, Peterborough, Lincoln, York and Durham, a distance of 420 miles, and thereby help promote the East Of England Heritage route. Apart from raising over £7,500 for the cathedral restoration funds by sponsors, the walk took me through an area of England neglected by many countryside lovers. Although the scenery was relatively flat and had no striking hills and dales, the area does have its own irresistible charm.

Before leaving Norwich on the first stage of the walk, I called at the Mustard Shop. Norwich is the birthplace of Colman's Mustard, started in 1804. The manager, dressed in a pin-stripe suit with a red carnation in his buttonhole, presented me with a pack of mustard bath preparation. 'Here', he said, 'this should be your warmest memories of the walk!' Rather than open the pack, I carried the yellow powder all the way to Durham.

I had pre-planned the walk and intended to camp out every night, except in the cities, which I did. Wherever possible, I wanted to use footpaths and bridleways, but except in a few isolated places the paths are little used. The stiles were often overgrown and the farmers had, because of lack of use, ploughed the paths out. A sad state of affairs, but a fact of life in areas away from National Parks and scenic areas. As a result I resorted to using country lanes, and had sore feet into the bargain.

Two days from Norwich I camped beside the River Ouse at Thetford. To my horror, in the morning the ground and trees were coated in thick ice and my pan of water inside the tent was frozen solid. Two hours later and I was walking through Thetford Forest, the second largest forest in England, occupying an area of 51,600 acres. Both mallard and moorhen took fright at my intrusion of their domain, and a grey heron, with its slow but powerful wing beats, left the water's edge as I approached. In the trees themselves, three green woodpeckers hammered away. Nearing Stanton Downham, the Forestry Commission base for the forest, a grey squirrel nonchalantly ran along the grass in front of me. In the village a garden gate bore this rhyme:-

> You may be early,
> You may be late,
> But please don't forget to shut the gate!

Eight miles from Ely I had to cross the River Lark at Isleham. To do so the Ely authorities had arranged for a traditional fenland gun punt to take me across. The boat belonged to Josh Scott, the Warden of the Wildfowl Trust Observatory at Welney. He poled me across the swift flowing river in this very shallow drafted boat. Originally, the hunter would lie full length on the deck and use his hands to propel the boat. Mounted on the boat would be a gun loaded with about a pound of shot. At one shot it was possible to kill about a dozen birds. Such cruelty is now a thing of the past. The boat was made of deal with a hardwood keel. To make it waterproof, pitch was poured into the interior.

Apse — Norwich Cathedral.

Walking into Isleham one hour later, I witnessed one of the most amazing sights of the fen country—a sunset. Just as at sea, the glowing ball descended into the ground. Ely Cathedral sits on a small prominence, and is often referred to as an island floating on a sea of land. Much of the surrounding area is barely above sea level. Having been drained, the land has sunk, leaving the roads a few feet above the dark rich soil. Despite the flat scene, the area is beautiful with only trees, hedges and dykes breaking the landscape and no stone walls. Walking to Peterborough, at one place I was 14 ft. below sea level. The birds were numerous in these quieter areas, with wren, robin thrush, goldfinch, skylark, yellowhammer, lapwing and pheasant seen every day. The hedgerows, although the cold weather was restricting growth, were alive with flowers. Most numerous were coltsfoot, white deadnettle, stitchwort, lesser celandine, primroses and clumps of lesser periwinkle, and wood anemones were coming into flower.

The halfway point of the walk was Lincoln, and on my four-day walk from Peterborough to there, I moved out of the fen country and passed through the more rolling countryside with small hills and depressions. For the first time I came across stone walls dividing the fields, which did appear odd. Just after leaving Peterborough I came to the delightful village of Helpston, whose main street consisted of attractive and well-looked-after thatched cottages. One bore a plaque to John Clare, the poet who was born here in 1793. Often referred to as 'the Northamptonshire peasant poet', he wrote prolifically, and the 'Village Minstrel' is probably his best known work. In his early forties he became insane and died in a lunatic asylum in 1864.

Almost midway between the two renowned coaching towns of Grantham and Stamford, I passed through the village of Woolsthorpe. The manor house, which is now owned by the National Trust, is where Sir Isaac Newton was born in 1642. The orchard is said to contain a descendant from the apple tree from which he observed the falling apple, which led to his discovery of the law of gravity.

Ely Cathedral.

Central Tower, West Front, from Lantern — Ely Cathedral.

Lincoln Cathedral.

York Cathedral — West Front.

West Towers, Durham Cathedral.

York-bound from Lincoln and en route for Gainsborough, I reached the village of Stow, whose cruciform church incorporates considerable amounts of both Saxon and Norman workmanship. On the green near the church was a relic of the past, whipping irons. The left hand one is believed to have been made by William Hill, the village blacksmith, in 1789. In days gone by, persons convicted of petty offences or brawling were often publicly whipped on market days. This was a very popular form of punishment in the 18th Century.

Entering the Isle of Axholme, another area drained and bordered by dykes and rivers, I came to Epworth, the renowned village of the Wesley family. John Wesley, the founder of Methodism, was born here on 17th June, 1703. The market cross bears a plaque to him, and from its steps he often preached to the assembled crowd. The town of Crowle, six miles north of Epworth, was the end of a day's walk. When I awoke the next morning, although now almost in April, the ground was covered with a four inch layer of snow. Such are the joys of solo long distance walking! You see the countryside in its various cloaks.

After York one entered a different world with hills for the first time. Heading for Durham meant walking between the two National Parks of the Yorkshire Dales and North York Moors. It was a strange sensation seeing these rise to 2,000 ft., with the Cleveland Hills on my right and Wensleydale on my left. The flowers became more abundant, with the river bank covered in butterbur. The birds too were more varied, and within the space of two minutes I spotted both a dipper and that fascinating bird, a kingfisher. In the fields curlew and lapwings cried and black-headed gulls followed in the wake of the farmer's tractor. Near the ruins of Jervaulx Abbey, a pair of snipe leapt up before me in their characteristic zig-zagged flight, and a couple of oystercatchers gazed on unperturbed.

Near Boroughbridge, I walked past the three tall upright stones known as the Devil's Arrows. Each weigh about 40 tons, and according to local legend they are crossbow bolts fired by the Devil at an early Christian settlement nearby. Apparently he missed! On my final night, I camped at Kirk Merrington eight miles south of Durham. That night the vicar recalled the story of the Kirk Merrington tragedy when, in the mid-18th Century, three children were cruelly murdered. The murderer was soon caught, and, as was the custom in those days, he was gibbeted. Instead of his body hanging in chains at the scene of the murder after he had been hung, he was hung alive. According to the tale his girlfriend fed him food from a stick until he died. I saw the children's grave the following day, and it bears the words 'Hung in chains'.

Originally, I was not supposed to reach Durham until 3.00 p.m., but I was walking too well to stop and linger and so arrived two hours early. Instead of making my presence known, I found a quiet inn where I could sit and come to terms with myself before the triumphant march to the cathedral door could begin. Soon after 3.00 p.m. I was welcomed by the Mayor and Dean before I clasped the historic Sanctuary Knocker as a symbol of the end of the walk. That night, in the very unfamiliar surroundings of a luxurious hotel, I undid the packet of mustard powder and wriggled my toes in the soothing liquid!

HERITAGE ROUTE

		Mileage	Overall Mileage

NORWICH TO ELY

Day 1   MAPS—1:50,000 O.S. Nos. 134 and 144 Norwich—A.140—Keswick—Intwood Hall—Monument Ketteringham—Stanfield Hall—High House Farm—Lower Wood—Ashwellthorpe—Fundenhall Street—Packway Farm—Bunwell Street—Carleton Rode—New Buckenham   21   21

Day 2   MAPS—1:50,000 O.S. No. 144 New Buckenham—Russell Lodge—Banham Moor—Quidenham—East Harling—Middle Harling—The Dower House—Fifty Acre Plantation—Thorpe Farm—Shadwell—Brettenham—Langmere Hill—Kilverstone Hall—Green Lane, Thetford   20   41

Day 3   MAPS—1:50,000 O.S. Nos. 144 and 143 Thetford—B.1107—New Plantation—Warren Wood—Little Lodge Farm—Santon Downham—Grimes Graves (Flint Mines)—Brandon—A1065—Wangford—Maidscross Hill—Lakenheath—Claypits—High Fen—Wilde Street—Back Row—Thistley Green—West Row—River Lark—Isleham   23   64

Day 4   MAPS—1:50,000 O.S. No. 143 Isleham—Soham Fen—Soham—Hainey Farm—Barway—Cawdle Fen—Laburnum House—Ely   10   74

ELY TO PETERBOROUGH:

Day 5   MAPS—1:50,000 O.S. Nos. 143 and 142 Ely—Thetford Corner—Little Thetford—Stretham—A.1123—Wilburton—Haddenham—Earith—Bluntisham—Colne—Somersham—Pidley—Oldhurst   22   96

Day 6   MAPS—1:50,000 O.S. No. 142 Oldhurst—Broughton—Wistow—Bury—Ramsey—Biggin—Lotting Fen—B.1040—Ramsey St. Mary's—Halfway Farm—Holme—Stilton—Yaxley—Pig Water—Farcet—River Nene—Horsey Hill and Civil War Fort—Stanground—Peterborough   22   118

Day 7   Peterborough

PETERBOROUGH TO LINCOLN

Day 8   MAPS—1:50,000 O.S. Nos. 142 and 130 Peterborough—Westwood—Marholm—Pellet Hall—Woodcroft Castle—Helpston—Bainton—Uffington—Uffington Old Wood—Essendine—Clay Hill—Pickworth—Pickworth Great Wood—Clipsham   22   140

Day 9   MAPS—1:50,000 O.S. No. 130 Clipsham—Addah Wood—Stocken Hall—South Witham—North Witham—Colsterworth—Crabtree House—Stoke Rochford Hall—Great Ponton—Little Ponton—Grantham   20   160

Day 10   MAPS—1:50,000 O.S. Nos. 130 and 121 Grantham—Belton House—Syston—Barkston—Carlton Ashes—Hough on the Hill—Caythorpe—Fulbeck—Leadenham—Welbourn—Wellingore—Navenby—Boothby Graffoe—Coleby—Harmston—Waddington—Bracebridge—Lincoln.   25   185

Day 11   Lincoln.

LINCOLN TO YORK:

Day 12   MAPS—1:50,000 O.S. No. 121 Lincoln—Burton—South Carlton—North Carlton—Toll Bridge Lane—Sturton by Stow—Stow—Willingham—Kexby—Upton—Walk Farm, Bass Wood—Gainsborough   20   205

Day 13   MAPS—1:50,000 O.S. No. 112 Gainsborough—River Trent—Walkerith—East Stockwith—Ravensfleet—Wildsworth—East Ferry—Owston Ferry—Epworth—Isle of Axeholme—Belton—Crowley Station—Crowle   20   225

Day 14	MAPS—1:50,000 O.S. Nos. 112 and 105 Crowle—Rainsbutt Ho.—Mount Pleasant—Swinefleet—Goole—Clifton Gardens—Boothferry Bridge—Knedlington—Asselby—Brackenholme—Hemingbrough	20	245
Day 15	MAPS—1:50,000 O.S. No. 105 Hemingbrough—River Ouse—Selby—Bondgate—Wistow—Cawood—Kelfield Grange—Stillingfleet—Moreby—Naburn—Acaster Malbis—River Ouse—York	21	266
Day 16	York		

YORK TO DURHAM:

Day 17	MAPS—1:50,000 O.S. No. 105 and 1" O.S. No. 91 York—Clifton—River Ouse—Nether Poppleton—River Ouse—Beningbrough—Beningbrough Park—Newton-on-Ouse—Linton-on-Ouse—Aldwark—Aldwark Grange—Myton on Swale—White Battle 1322 A.D.—Ellenthorpe—Boroughbridge	22	288
Day 18	MAPS—1" O.S. No. 91 Boroughbridge—Skelton—Ripon—Gooseberry—Piney Moor Wood—Burntroots Plantation—Greenass Farm—Grewelthorpe—River Ure—Masham	20	308
Day 19	MAPS—1" O.S. No. 91 Masham—River Ure—Squirrel Bank—Jervaulx Abbey—River Ure—Illshaw Bridge—Swarble Hill—Stoop House—Cross Lane House—Barden—Half-penny House—Barden Fell—Hipswell Moor—Middle Moor—Holly Hill—Richmond	21	329
Day 20	MAPS—1" O.S. Nos. 91 and 85 Richmond—Skeeby—A.1—Scuttagh House—Moulton—Middleton Tyas—Barton—Newton Morrell—Jolby Manor—Stapleton Manor—Blackwell—Darlington—Harrowgate Village—Whessoe—Coatham Mundeville—Hill House—Neighington Station—Stockton—Darlington Railway—Shildon	24	353
Day 21	MAPS—1" O.S. No. 85 Shildon—Old Eldon—Howlish Hall—Coundon—Westerton—Middlestone Moor—Spennymoor—Burton Beck Farm—Woodhouse Farm—River Wear—Sunderland Bridge—Croxdale Wood House—River Wear—Durham	17	370
Day 22	Durham and return home—by train!		

The walk was 370 miles on paper but 420 miles on the ground.

West Front — Peterborough Cathedral.

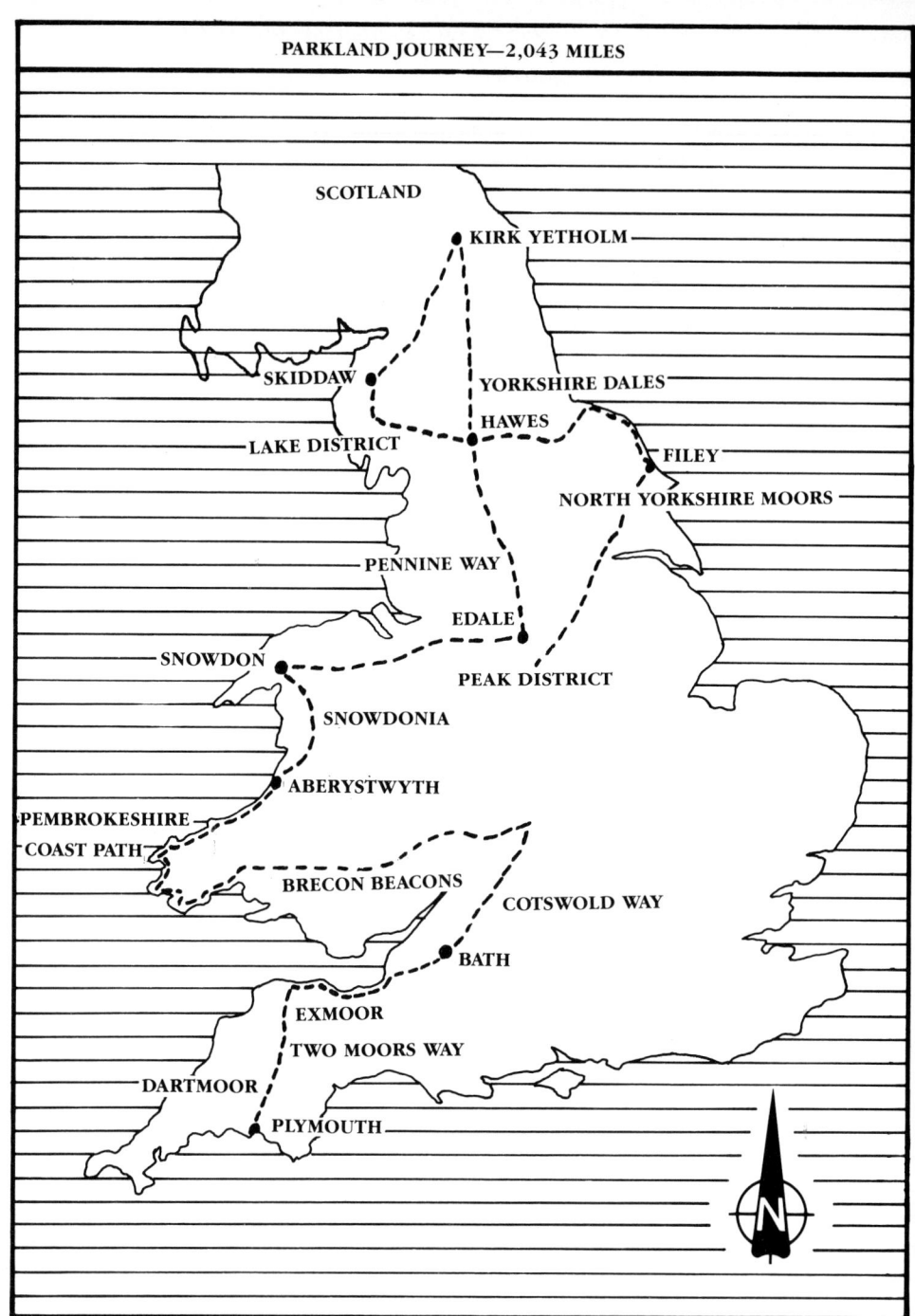

PARKLAND JOURNEY

Imagine walking through all our ten National Parks in one walk—along stunning coastlines; ascending high, rugged and remote mountains; exploring picturesque villages; and seeing a wealth of wild flowers and animals. Sounds a dream, but during the summer of 1976 I had the good fortune to do this. In the space of 84 days I walked 2,043 miles and, apart from four days when it rained, I had continuous sunshine. With the bare essentials of life on my back—tent, sleeping bag, spare clothes and cooking equipment—I set off from Plymouth in late May to walk and see at first hand our countryside.

My first destination was Dartmoor via Plym Forest. The days were idyllic with few people about and the full flush of spring flowers carpeting the ground. The river banks were bursting with gorse and broom blossom, while the neighbouring fields were ablaze with bluebells. I climbed the rocky tors and gazed down at the view of villages, reservoirs, woodland and moors. Descending Bellever Tor I saw several ponies and their foals. A sight to gladden the heart of any wanderer. After three days it was with regret that I left the National Park and walked through the woodland around Fingle Bridge and Castle Drogo, before descending to the thatched village of Drewsteignton. On the way I surprised a couple of roe deer, and a green woodpecker kept flying ahead of me.

To reach Exmoor, my next park, I crossed delightful undulating countryside, passing through many thatched villages and quiet leafy lanes. Part of the time I followed the Moors Way, a long distance footpath linking Dartmoor and Exmoor together. I found Exmoor to be not so rugged as Dartmoor, but with many secluded stretches of moorland. Two days later I walked into Lynton on Bank Holiday Monday. The contrast from quiet moorland to crowds of people was unbearable. I was short of food, but I was so put off by seeing so many people that I only purchased two items and fled. I settled down later and camped at Porlock with a sweeping view of the curved bay.

I continued around the coast, often 500 ft. above the sea, to Minehead and Watchet. Nearing Minehead and the boundary of the National Park, the cliffs, being early June, were adorned with rhododendrons whose purple flowers radiated out against a backcloth of blue sea. From Watchet I headed inland and crossed the Quantock Hills. This small detached group of hills are always a joy to ascend on clear paths. Their summits provide exceptional vantage points over the coast and eastwards to Cheddar and the Mendips.

Walking through Bridgwater I came to Cheddar Gorge and marvelled at the steep limestone buttresses towering above me. Next I passed through the Mendip Hills to Bath. This area came as a complete surprise, being really attractive rural countryside, full of picturesque villages and reservoirs. In time I reached Bath, with more than 300 miles walked. I never tire of visiting Bath, with its beautiful Abbey and rich carvings; the Georgian buildings and Roman Baths all combine to make it an exceptional place. I arrived at the right time, on a Saturday morning, when a team of Morris Dancers from Warminster danced to the delight of an ever-increasing crowd. This was England at its best; the old traditions being kept alive. I left the forecourt of the Abbey to begin walking the Cotswold Way, and, as I did so, I came across another team of Morris Dancers.

John Merrill on the Pembrokeshire coast.

The Cotswold Way traverses the western edge of the Cotswold Hills, from Bath to Chipping Campden, and is 100 miles long. The four days I spent walking the route through scenic countryside and mellow-stoned villages was some of the finest walking of the whole route. Clear signposts ensure that you never stray. Very surprisingly, I only met two other walkers walking the Way, and they in a north to south direction. All the time I had a magnificent view westwards of the River Severn and the South Wales hills. The villages leave you spellbound. Two of the most unforgettable were Broadway and Stanton. Chipping Campden is equally as fine, and makes a fitting end to the route.

From the Cotswolds I turned westwards through the Vale of Evesham to the Malvern Hills. Evesham came as a delightful surprise, and an area I would love to explore more fully. The Malvern Hills are more dramatic than the Quantocks. Again they are a magnificent walk along a fine ridge with incredible distant views in all directions. Leaving this mountain barrier behind, I descended to Ledbury and its gabled houses, and walked on to the Brecon Beacons. Possibly not one of the better-known National Parks, apart from the Beacons area, it is nevertheless one of great character and interest. Flanking the popular Beacons are the Black Mountains. Here there are few paths, and it is perfect for the more adventurous walker, experienced in map reading. My crossing of these mountains was among the remotest walking country I walked in.

Beyond the Black Mountains I slipped through Carmarthen to reach Amroth and the start of the Pembrokeshire Coast Path. Again this is another of those paths which, apart from certain areas, is not often walked in its entirety. I am baffled why, for the coastline—168 miles of it to Poppit Sands near Cardigan—is quite exceptional. I only met two others walking it, and again in a north to south direction. I have walked the Path three times now, and still marvel at its beauty. Many expanses of golden sands, sheer cliffs exposing perfect examples of rock folds, numerous nesting sea birds and beautiful places such as the Bosherton lily ponds are part of every day's walk. For the first time in almost a month, it rained. In the space of eight hours one inch of rain fell, leaving me drenched. The next day was perfect—blue sky, hot sun and good clarity. Six weeks were to pass before it rained again!

After Poppit Sands I continued up another 50 miles of coastline to Aberystwyth, before heading to Cader Idris and Snowdonia. The contract of rugged coastline to the high, sheer mountains was magical. The sun, now in late June, was overpowering. On the coast it was twenty degrees cooler than in the mountains. The force of the sun soon upset my schedule. 1,000 ft. up on Snowdon the temperature was well into the nineties. To overcome this and still climb all the main mountains—Snowdon, the Glyders and Carnedds—I set off at 4.00 a.m. and was on the summits three hours later. From 10.30 onwards the heat was oppressive, and it took me seven hours to walk 10 miles! To keep cool I swam in every river and mountain lake that I came to. This was enjoying nature at its best.

After ascending the Carnedds I left Snowdonia behind and wove my way through the Midlands, skirting the Potteries, to the Peak District National Park. All the National Parks have their own unique character, and the Peak District is no exception with its gritstone edges, limestone dales, and moorland plateaus. At Edale I joined the Pennine Way, which I walked in its entirety, in two halves, using Hawes in the Yorkshire Dales as the terminus. This was so that I could walk in a clockwise direction and walk through the Lake District and North Yorkshire Moors.

Vine Street, Winchcombe, Cotswolds.

High Force, River Tees, Teesdale.

The Pennine Way occupies a unique place in the walking scene of Britain. I had refrained from walking it up to this point because of its popularity. As you can see, on the other long—distance walks I met only a couple walking. Here, on the Pennine Way, between 50 and 70 people were passed each day. In many ways it can be described as a walker's motorway. But the route through the Pennines to Kirk Yetholm can only be described as matchless. After four days' walking I reached Hawes and turned left for the Lake District, following part of the Dales Way to Bowness in Windermere.

Like the Pennine Way, the Lake District casts its spell on any traveller. Those high mountains, deep valleys and lakes command respect and admiration. If I had to choose between the Lake District and Snowdonia I would be at a loss to do so. Both are marvellous mountain areas full of their own distinctive style. To maintain my theme of climbing all the highest mountains, I ascended the Langdale Pikes, Scafell Pike, Great Gable and finally Cat Bells before descending to Keswick. Heading northwards with 1,400 miles walked, I reached Carlisle via Skiddaw. It felt strange being in border country, and after following the early part of Hadrians Wall I headed northwards to Kielder Forest and the northern end of the Pennine Way.

Kielder Forest and Northumberland are our remotest area of English countryside. For two days I crossed through secluded mountains and moorlands, meeting no one! Just me, my map and compass and nature. I saw a pair of roe deer and a fawn nonchalantly ate some leaves while I watched entranced from 20 ft. Beyond Kielder Forest I gained Bryness in the Northumberland National Park, and walked into Scotland to Kirk Yetholm, my most northern point.

Heading southwards, as though descending, I followed the Pennine Way back to Hawes in the Yorkshire Dales. I was sorry to leave it, and for the first time I knew I was on the final stages of the walk. I walked through Wensleydale and out into the Yorkshire Plain to Thirsk and finally Helmsley, the starting point of the Cleveland Way around the North Yorkshire Moors. It is only 100 miles long, and is one of the most perfect routes imaginable. The first 50 miles is through the Hambleton Hills and moors to Saltburn by the Sea, and the remainder is along the east coast via Whitby and Scarborough to Filey. A perfect balance between mountain and coastal scenery. I indulged in many swims from the now crowded beaches, for it was mid-August, as I walked down the coast.

Rather sad and alarmed at the waiting media, I walked into Filey a day ahead of schedule after walking 1,897 miles in 78 days. I slipped quietly away the next morning to walk through the Yorkshire Wolds to my home in the Peak District. The five day walk of 150 miles gave me time to reflect on what I had achieved and seen. The memories were too full of beautiful sights. I was indeed a lucky man. I reached home convinced of two things. Firstly, to really appreciate our countryside you must get out and walk, for it will make you a richer person. Secondly, encompassed in so small an area we have a very diverse range of scenery which nowhere else can equal.

SOME BRIEF FACTS OF 'PARKLAND JOURNEY'— SUMMER OF 1976

The walk lasted 84 days—from 27th May to 18th August inclusive.

A distance of 2,043 miles was walked—an average of about 25 miles per day.

The walk linked together the ten National Parks of England and Wales. In walking order they were—Dartmoor, Exmoor, Brecon Beacons, Pembrokeshire Coast, Snowdonia, Peak District, Yorkshire Dales, Lake District, Northumberland, and North Yorkshire Moors.

Encompassed in the walk were the total lengths of four long distance footpaths—The Cotswold Way, Pembrokeshire Coast Footpath, Pennine Way, and the Cleveland Way. Sections of other major footpaths were crossed, and these included the S.W. Peninsula Footpath, Peakland Way, Moors Way, Dales Way and Wolds Way. I also climbed all the highest mountains of England and Wales and crossed the remotest areas of countryside.

I walked alone carrying the bare necessities of life on my back, and my rucksack and cameras together weighed 60 lbs.

During the 84-day walk I spent
    74 nights under canvas
    2 nights at Bed and Breakfast, and
    8 nights in Youth Hostels.

I ate— 464 bars of chocolate
          40 lbs. of sugar
          drank 152 pints of milk
          put on 5 lbs. in weight
          took 1,600 colour slides, and 1,000 black/white photographs.

Out of 84 days, only on four days did it rain. One particular day one inch of rain fell in 8 hours!

48 maps needed for Parkland journey.

PARKLAND JOURNEY— ORIGINAL PLAN

Day	1:50,000 O.S. Map	Route	Mileage	Overall Mileage
1	201 & 202	The Citadel (Plymouth)—River Plym—Longbridge—Plym—Plym Forest—Bickleigh—Goodameavy—River Meavy—Callisham Down—Meavy—Burrator Reservoir—Sheepstor.	15	15
2	202 & 191	Sheepstor—Ditsworthy Warren—Nuns Cross Farm—Sherberton—Dunnabridge Pound—Bellever Tor—Clapper Bridge (Postbridge)—East Dart River—Grey Wethers—Fernworthy Reservoir—Collihole—Chagford.	20	35
3	191	Chagford—River Teign—Hunter's Tor—Drewsteignton—Vete Mill—Forder Farm—Hittisleigh Cross—Hittisleigh Barton—Nymetwood—Blue Violet—Hilldown—Nymet Tracey—Bow—Tuckingmill—Zeal Monachorum—Stopgate Cross—Kelland Cross—Lapford.	17	52
4	191 & 180	Lapford—Forches Cross—Handsford Farm—Fiddlecott—B3042—Chawleigh—Hollow Tree Cross—Little Dart River—Chulmleigh—Brookland—Challacombe—Measbury Moor—Romansleigh—Alswear—South Molton—East Marsh—River Mole—North Molton.	20	72
5	180	North Molton—Heasley Mill—Span Head—Comerslade—Mole's Chamber—Bill Hill Stone—Saddlegate—East Ilkerton—Barbrook—Lynton.	17	89
6	180 & 181	Lynton—Coast Path—Foreland Point—Countisbury Cove—Glenthorne—Culbone—Worthy—Porlock Bay—Hurlstone Point—Eastern Brockholes—Minehead.	18	107
7	181	Minehead—Blue Anchor Bay—Watchet—Doniford—West Wood—Staple—Beacon Hill—Black Ball Hill—Crowcombe Park Gate—Quantock Combe.	18	125
8	181 & 182	Quantock Combe—Aley—Halseycross Farm—Radlet—Spaxton—Four Forks—Rexworthy Farm—Durleigh Reservoir—Bridgwater—A39—Sydenham Manor—Horsey—Bawdrip—Cossington—Chilton Polden.	18	143
9	182	Chilton Polden—Chilton Moor—Burtle Hill—River House—Westham—Blackford—Washbrook—Brinscombe Hill—River Yeo—Cheddar Reservoir—Cheddar—Cheddar Gorge—Gorsey Bigbury—Lower Ellick Farm—Butcombe.	19	162
10	172	Butcombe—Ridgehill—Pagans Hill—Chew Magna—Stanton Drew—Pensford—Publow—Woolard—Compton Dando—Burnett—Corston—Bath.	18	180
11	172 & 173	Bath—(Cotswold Way)—Kelston Round Hill—Landsdown Hill—The Battlefields—Pennsylvania—Dyrham—Dodington Park—Little and Old Sodburys—Horton—Hawksbury Monument—Lower Kilcott—Alderley.	20	200
12	172 & 173	(Cotswold Way) Alderley—Wortley Hill—Tor Hill—& Wotton-under-Edge—Brackenburg Ditches—N. Nibley Monument—Stinchcombe Hill—Dursley—Cam Long Down—Uleybury—Frocester Hill—Ryeford.	20	220

13	163	(Cotswold Way) Ryeford—Dove Row Hill—Maiden Hill—Randwick—Haresfield Beacon—Scotsquar—Painswick—Paradise—Coopers Hill—Witcombe Woods—The Peak—Crickley Hill—Ullenwood.	20	240
14	163	(Cotswold Way) Ullenwood—Leckhampton Hill—Charlton Common—Seven Springs—Dowdeswell Res.—Piccadilly—Cleeve Hill—Belas Knap—Winchcombe—Hailes Abbey—Stanway.	20	260
15	150 & 151	(Cotswold Way) Stanway—Stanton—Shenberrow Camp—Broadway—Broadway Hill—Dover's Hill—Chipping Campden.	20	280
16	151 & 150	Chipping Campden—Saintbury Hill—Willersley—Wickhamford—Evesham—Charlton—Fladbury—Wyre Piddle—Pershore.	20	300
17	150	Pershore—Defford—Marsh Common—Baughton—Upton-upon—Severn—Hanley Castle—Hanley Swan—Malvern Hills (Nr. Little Malvern).	17	317
18	150 & 149	Little Malvern—Herefordshire Beacon—The Gullet—Ledbury Flights Farm—Little Marcle—Marcle Hill—Woolhope—Haugh Wood—Even Pits—Holme Lacy.	21	338
19	149 & 161	Holme Lacy—Ramsden Coppice—Nether Wood—Aconbury—Kingsthorne—Much Dewchurch—Kilpeck—Cross Llyde—Pontrilas Rowlstone—Mynydd Merddin—Clodock.	20	358
20	161 & 160	Clodock—Llanthony—Mynydd Ddu Forest—Cwm Farm—Pen Allt—Mawr—Cwmdu—Half-Way Inn—Coed-Yr-Ynys—Cwm Crawnon—Talybont Reservoir—Nant Tarthwyni.	22	380
21	160	Nant Tarthwyni—Craigy Fan—Craig Cwm—Oergwm—Cribin—Pen Y Fan—Corn Du—Storey Arms—Fan Fawr—Ystradfellte Reservoir—Mellte Castle—Blaen—Nedd—Isaf.	18	398
22	160 & 159	Blaen—Nedd—Isaf—Sand Hill—Penwyllt—Gwyn Arms—Disgwylfa—Carnau Nant—Menyn—Gareg Las—Tyle Du—Carn—Pen-Y-Clogau—Pant Nant—Fforchog—Tair Carn Isaf—The Forge.	21	419
23	159	The Forge—Blaengweche—Derwydd—Temple Bar—Gilfach Pen-Pal—Penallt—Garn-Wen—The Park Farm—Erw-Wen—Carmarthen.	22	441
24	159 & 158	Carmarthen—Llanllwch—Wernddu—Penplas—Llangynog—Croes-y-Ceiliog—Pont Ddu—Trig Point 60—St. Clears—New Mill—Castell Toch—Marros—Amroth.	22	463
25	158	Amroth—Pembrokeshire Coast Path—Saundersfoot—Tenby—Giltar Point—Lydstep Haven—Manorbier—Swanlake Bay.	18	481
26	158	Swanlake Bay—Freshwater East—Barafundle Bay—Bosherton—St. Govan's Head—Flimston Bay—Castlemartin—Freshwater West—Angle.	20	501
27	157	Angle—Pembroke River—Pembroke—Neyland Bridge—Milford Haven—Sandy Haven.	22	523
28	157	Sandy Haven—Dale—St. Ann's Head—Westdale Bay—Marloes Sands—Martin's Haven.	21	544
29	157	Martin's Haven—Musselwick Sands—The Nab Head—Little Haven—Broad Haven—Nolton Haven—Newgale Sands—Solva.	24	568

30	157	Solva—St. Non's Bay—Ramsey Sound—Whitesands Bay—Abereiddy—Trevine.	24	592
31	157	Trevine—Abercastle—Strumble Head—Carregwastad Point—Goodwick—Fishguard—Castle Point.	23	615
32	157 & 145	Castle Point—Dinas Head—Newport—Ceibwr Bay.	18	633
33	145	Ceibwr Bay—Camaes Head—Poppit Sands—Cardigan—Verwig—Llwnysgaw—Aberporth.	18	651
34	145 & 146	Aberporth—Tresaith—Llangranog—Newquay—Aberaeron.	20	671
35	146 & 135	Aberaeron—Llansantffraid—Llanrhystud—Coastline to Aberystwyth.	18	689
36	135	Aberystwyth—Bow Street—Old Mine—Bontgoch—Winllan—Moel-y-Llyn—Glaspwll—Machynlleth.	21	710
37	135 & 124	Machynlleth—Maes-y-Wern-Goch—Tarren Gesdil—Cedris—Cader Idris—Gwernan Lake Hotel—Dolgellau.	18	728
38	124	Dolgellau—Llanfachreth—Coed Y Brenin Forest—Trawslynydd—Ffestiniog.	21	749
39	124 & 115	Ffestiniog—Pen-Y-Cefn—Tanygrisiau—Llyn Y Adar—Nantgwynant—Watkin Path—Snowdon—Crib Goch—Pen Y Pass.	18	767
40	115	Pen Y Pass—Glyder Fawr—Llyn Idwal—Ogwen—Carnedd Dafydd—Carnedd Llywelyn—Cwm Eigiau—Siglen—Trefriw.	20	787
41	115 & 116	Trefriw—Llanrwst—Melin-Y-Coed—Oerfa—Llwyn Saint—Gors Dopiog—Nant Bach—Llyn Bran.	18	805
42	116	Llyn Bran—AAfod Caradoc—Rhwng-Y-Ddwy-Afon—Cyffylliog—The Mill—Galltegfa—Ruthin—Bathafarn Farm—Moelgyw—Four Crosses.	19	824
43	116 & 117	Four Crosses—Pen-Y-Coed—Talwrn—Trewddyn—Hores—Hope—Shordley Hall—Burton Green—Pulford.	18	842
44	117	Pulford—Aldford—Gatesheath—Newton—Beeston—Bunbury Calveley.	19	861
45	118	Calveley—Brooklands Farm—Church Minshull—Warmingham—Elworth—Sandbach—Martin's Moss—Brownlow Heath—Little Moreton Hall—Canal.	19	880
46	118 & 119	Canal—Mow Cop—Biddulph Lask Edge—Horton—Leek—Benthead—Onecote—Ford—Grindon—Manifold Valley—Wetton Mill.	20	900
47	1" O.S. 'Peak Dist' Tourist Map	Wetton Mill—(Peakland Way)—Hulme End—Brund—Longnor—Earl Sterndale—Horseshoe Dale—Deep Dale—Chee Dale—Wormhill—Peter Dale—Hay Dale—Dam Dale—Peak Forest—Old Moor—Rowter Farm.	21	921
48	1" O.S. 'Peak Dist' Tourist Map	Rowter Farm—Mam Tor—Hollins Cross—Edale—(Pennine Way)—Grindsbrook—Kinder Scout—Kinder Downfall—Mill Hill—Snake Road—Devil's Dike—Bleaklow Head—Clough Edge—Crowden.	20	941
49	1" O.S. 'Peak Dist' Tourist Map 101 & 105	Crowden—Laddow Rocks—Crowden Great Brook—Black Hill—Wessenden Head Moor—White Moss—Black Moss Reservoir—Standedge—Close Moss—A640—Rapes Hill—White Hill—Windy Hill—Blackstone Edge—White House Inn—Regulating Drain—Light Hazzles Reservoir—Warland Reservoir.	20	961

50	95 & 1" O.S.	Warland Reservoir—Mankin Holes YHA—Stoodley Pike—Callis Wood—A646—Colden—Heptonstall Moor—Walshaw Dean Reservoir—Withins—The Height—Ponden Reservoir—Wold Stones—Ickornshaw Moor—Lumb.	21	982
51	95 & 90 1" O.S.	Lumb—Ickornshaw—Lothersdale—Elsack Moor—Thornton in Craven—East Marton—Gargrave—Eshton Moor—(Yorkshire Dales N.P.)—Airton—Hanlith Bridge—Malham.	20	1,002
52	90 & 1" O.S.	Malham—Gordale Scar—Malham Cove—Malham Tarn—Tennant Gill—Fountains Fell—Rainscar—Pen-y-Ghent—Hull Pot—Horton in Ribblesdale—Jackdaw Hole—Old Ing—Cam Beck.	20	1,022
53	90 & 1" O.S.	Cam Beck—Cam End—Cam High Road—Hawes—Widdale—Dent Fell—Lea Yeat—Dentdale.	20	1,042
54	90 & 89 1" O.S.	Dentdale—Dent—R. Dee—Holme Fell—Tarn Moss—New Hutton—Kendal.	18	1,060
55	89 & 1" O.S. Lake Dist. Tourist	Kendal—Cold Harbour—Beckside—Crook Hall—Gilpin Park Plantation—Bowness on Windermere—Ferry—Far Sawrey—Esthwaite Water—Hawkshead.	18	1,087
56	1" O.S. Lake Dist. Tourist	Hawkshead—Tarn Hows—Lake Holme Fell—Little Langdale Tarn—Langdales—Langdale Pikes—Angle Tarn.	18	1,096
57	"	Angle Tarn—Esk Hawse—Scafell Pike—Scafell—Wasdale Head—Black Said Pass—Pillar—Ennerdale	18	1,114
58	"	Ennerdale—Red Pike—Buttermere—Crag Hill—Grisedale Pike—Braithwaite—Keswick.	17	1,131
59	82 & 83 1" O.S. Lake Dist.	Keswick—Skiddaw—Uldale Fells—Longlands—Caldbeck—Rosley.	18	1,149
60	1" O.S 83 & 76	Rosley—Dalston—Carlisle—Hadrian's Wall—Newtown—Kirkcambeck.	20	1,169
61	1" O.S. 76 & 70	Kirkcambeck—Bewcastle—Kershope Forest—Larriston Fells—Kielder Forest—Kielder Head.	18	1.187
62	1" O.S. & 70	Kielder Head—White Kielder Burn—Girdle Fell—Catcleugh Reservoir—Harry's Pike—Hungry Low—Leithope Forest—Upper Hindhope—Tow Ford—Humblemoor Hill—Greenhill.	20	1,207
63	70	Greenhill—The Street—Hall Burn—Bowmont Water—Primside Mill—Kirk Yetholm (Pennine Way)—Halterburn—Black Hag—The Schil—Auchope Cairn.	18	1,225
64	70 & 71	Auchope Cairn—Cairn Hill—The Cheviot—King's Seat—Russell's Cairn—Lamb Hill—Scraesburgh Fell—Brownhart Low—Ravens Knowe—Byrness.	20	1,245
65	70 & 77 1" O.S.	Byrness—Redesdale Forest—Padon Hill—Lord's Shaw—Lough Shaw—Abbey Rigg—Hareshaw Linn—Bellingham—Houxty Burn.	21	1,266
66	77 & 76 1" O.S.	Houxty Burn—Shitlington Crag—Warks Burn—Wark Forest—Stone Folds—Housesteads Crags—Hadrian's Wall—Milecastle 39/46.	21	1,287
67	1" O.S. 76 & 83	Milecastle 46—Thirlwall Castle—A69—Black Hill—Wain Rigg—Round Hill—Ulpham—Lambley Colliery—The Maiden Way—Burnstones—Slaggyford—Kirkaugh—River South Tyne.	21	1,308

68	1" O.S. 84 & 85	River South Tyne—Garrigill—Pikeman Hill—Long Man Hill—Cross Fell—Little Dun Fell—Great Dun Fell—Knock Fell—Swindale Beck—Halsteads Farm—Dufton.	18	1,326
69	1" O.S. 84 & 85	Dufton—Peeping Hill—High Cup—Maize Beck—Cauldron Snout—River Tees—Cronkley Bridge—High Force—River Tees.	20	1,346
70	84	River Tees—Wythes Hill Farm—Grass Holme Reservoir—Mickleton Moor—Blackton Reservoir—Deepdale Beck—Goldsborough—Levy Pool—Bowes—Wytham Moor—Sleightholme Moor—Tan Hill—Lad Gill.	20	1,366
71	84 & 90	Lad Gill—Low Firth Farm—Keld—Thwaite—Gt. Shunner Fell—Black Hill Moss—Hardrow—Hawes—Askrigg.	20	1,386
72	90 & 91 1" O.S.	Askrigg—Astgarth—West Burton—Middleham High Moor—Middleham Low Moor—Middleham—Jervaulx Abbey—River Ure.	20	1,406
73	91	River Ure—Charlcot—Watlass Moor House—Well—Kirklington—Skipton on Swale—Thirsk.	20	1,426
74	1" Tourist Ed. 'North Yorks Moors'	Thirsk—Bagby—Kilburn—Oldsteads—Wass—Wass Moor—Duncombe Park—Helmsley.	16	1,442
75	"	Helmsley—(Cleveland Way)—Duncombe Park—Rievaulx Abbey—Sutton Bank—Hambleton Hills—Black Hambleton.	20	1,462
76	"	Black Hambleton—Osmotherley—Near Moor—Live Moor—Cringle Moor—Hasty Bank—Ingleby Moor—Kildale.	19	1,481
77	"	Kildale—Great Ayton Moor—North Roseberry Topping—Hutton Moor—Scapewath Bridge—Airy Hill Farm—Skelton—Saltburn-by-the-Sea—Coastline to Boulby.	18	1,499
78	"	Boulby—(Coastline)—Staithes—Runswick—Kettleness—Sandsend—Whitby—Saltwick Bay—Robin Hood's Bay—Ravenscar.		
79	"	Ravenscar—Hayburn Wyke—Cloughton Wyke—Scarborough—Cayton Sands—Lebberston Cliff—North Cliff—Filey Brigg—Filey.	21	1,540

NOTE: On paper the whole walk is estimated to be—1,540 miles long, BUT on the ground the total mileage will be in excess of 1,800 miles. (1,000 miles on paper is generally 1,200 miles on location.) The walk in fact to Filey was 1,897 miles.

Suggested further reading—
Turn Right at Lands End John N. Merrill JNM Publications 1985
Twenty Years A-Growing Maurice O'Sullivan Oxford University Press 1983
The Aran Islands Daphne Pochin Mould David & Charles 1972
Islands of Ireland Donald McCormick Osprey 1974
The Islands of Ireland Thomas H. Mason Batsford 1950
The Mountains of England and Wales George Bridge West Col 1973
Ramblers' Ways Edited by David Sharp David & Charles 1980
Britain's National Parks Edited by Mervyn Bell David & Charles 1979
The Footpaths of Britain M. Marriott Queen Anne Press 1981

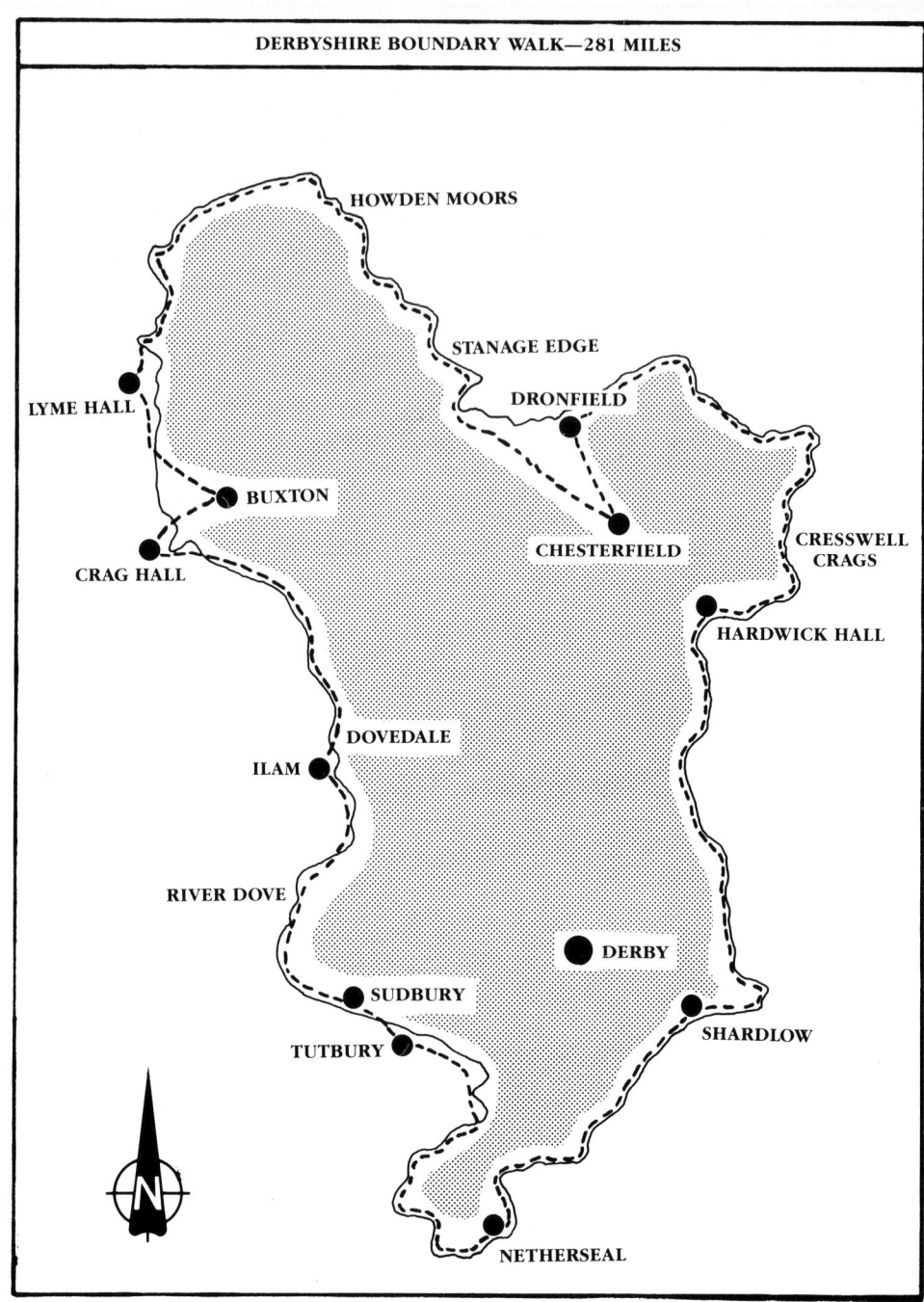

MY BOUNDARY WALK

I stood in a chamber room of Hardwick Hall, oblivious to the chatting crowd, as I sipped a glass of white wine. Everyone was immaculately dressed, whereas I, although the guest of honour, felt conspicuous in a sweat-stained open-necked shirt, a pair of shorts, and muddy boots on my feet! Yet I enjoyed the occasion, and, feeling like Billy Bunter, kept eyeing the mouth-watering strawberries soon to be served. I had two helpings! Just as well, as I had 32 miles to walk that afternoon. This was one of the more unusual aspects of my 281-mile walk around my county boundary during July 1977.

Just after completing a 2,000 mile walk during the summer of 1976, I was invited to a National Trust party at Ilam Hall. For a long while I had wanted to walk my county boundary, as much of it can be done using footpaths. I had decided I would do the walk in three weeks' time. At the party, again while I was drinking white wine, I met and chatted to David Garnett, the Regional Agent for the National Trust. During the conversation I mentioned my plan to walk the boundary in two weeks' time. Why not, he suggested, do it for our Derbyshire and Peak District Appeal Fund? I agreed to postpone the walk and do it next year (1977).

By Christmas 1976, the walk was given the go-ahead by the Appeal Committee, and planning began. It was agreed that the walk should start and end at Sudbury Hall, to coincide with the Sudbury Festival. Basing the end of the walk on Sunday, July 24th, (the last day of the Festival), I worked backwards and planned the start for Thursday, July 14th. The whole walk schedule was totally pre-planned three months ahead. I would walk clockwise around the boundary, calling at all the National Trust properties en route. Surprisingly, they all happen to be on or close to the boundary. It was also decided to include Lyme Hall, being both National Trust property and within the Peak District National Park, but outside Derbyshire.

I did leave the actual boundary on several occasions, but this was to fit in publicity events and fund-raising projects. I little realised just what I was letting myself in for, with so much to cram in each day plus walking 28 to 34 miles. It was, to say the least, more than an endurance test. Despite this, it was an enjoyable and unforgettable experience.

I had requested that it would be better for me to camp on National Trust property. Consequently, late on the Wednesday night I pitched the tent on the lawn of Sudbury Hall. I awoke to see the sun streaming through the tent—a good omen I thought. At first little seemed to be happening. Suddenly everything slotted into place. The landrover with ceremonial arch arrived to have its sign-writing put on. Schoolchildren arrived to be dressed in 18th Century costumes. The Press, B.B.C Radio Derby and both B.B.C. Midlands Today and A.T.V. film crews arrived. By now I had butterflies, and I wished I was on Kinder or Bleaklow rather than face the cameras! However, all went well. The Duchess of Devonshire saw me off, and with the noise of the children cheering in my ears I descended the steps and started the first stage of the walk to Ilam Hall.

I felt rather off-balance from such a send-off, but I calmed down once three miles were behind me. After eight miles walking via Doveridge, I reached Rocester. Here the ceremonial arch was erected in a conspicuous place. The locals cheered as I walked through! The pattern of the walk started to unfold. A lunchtime halt was arranged so that we could meet the locals, collect money and generally promote the Appeal. After an hour I heaved my 40 lb. pack onto my back and set off via Norbury and Mayfield to Ilam. One further halt was planned before I arrived there, as both B.B.C. Radio Sheffield and Radio Derby were following the walk. Finding a farmhouse at Church Mayfield, I used their 'phone to go out live on the radio. This was done every day in the late afternoon, and caused considerable problems finding a telephone.

Towards 7.30 p.m. I walked into Ilam and through the arch. A wine and cheese party was arranged, and I joined the throng. Yes, I had another glass of wine in my hand! Not my usual routine for a marathon walk, but I wasn't complaining! It was 11.30 p.m. before I put the tent up near the River Manifold, and in the darkness I cooked myself a meal. Apart from six bars of chocolate and glasses of wine, I hadn't eaten since breakfast.

The next morning the weather was at its best as I walked up Dovedale with a sponsored member of the Ashbourne Rotary Club. He, like many other Rotary Club members in the county, had been sponsored to walk a five-mile stretch with me. From Hartington I hurried on to Hollinsclough before ascending to Flash and down to Three Shires Head. The weather was so hot that on reaching the river Dane I found a deep pool. Without hesitation I stripped and dived in. It was beautifully refreshing, but on getting out the midges descended and bit furiously. Dressed, I continued on to Crag Hall, Lord Derby's shooting lodge. Another wine and cheese party was arranged in my honour with some 200 guests.

I arrived at the appointed hour of 7.30 p.m. However, as hardly any of the guests had arrived I hid in a nearby field. Finding a tall sycamore tree, I scaled the lower branches and through my binoculars could see everyone arriving! When the majority of people had gathered, I descended the tree and walked down the road and into the grounds. I approached the assembled crowd looking falsely tired from my non-stop walk! There was a sting in the tail to the day. I had not eaten, and did not eat until well past midnight. I slept on the lawn of the lodge and had breakfast with the gamekeeper!

Crag Hall, Wildboarclough, Shutlingsloe in background.

The third day was another testing one. From Crag Hall I crossed the moorland to Buxton to meet the Mayor, Mrs. Millican, and have lunch with her before walking in the Buxton Carnival. With the escort vehicle behind and a loud hailer voicing my walk, I felt decidedly out of place as I walked along the crowded streets. Fortunately I had only about half the route to do before I left and headed to the Goyt Valley via Burbage. Once past Windgather Rocks I climbed out of Kettleshulme via Bow Stones to reach Lyme Hall in the early evening. No party tonight, but a wine bottle was soon passed around. My usual diet is milk and chocolate on a walk, and I was rather worried as to how I would react to this new form of nourishment.

Leaving Lyme Hall the next day, I saw several red deer. My route lay over Mellor Moor and onto Chisworth and Tintwistle (Tinsel, as the locals call it). At first the weather was dry but cloudy. By lunchtime it was definitely overcast, and a downpour seemed imminent. Ahead was the toughest part of the walk over the moorland to Black Hill and Holme Moss. As I started, the heavens opened. In no time I was soaked to the skin, walking by compass across waterlogged terrain with the low cloud swirling around. I walked into Holme Moss T.V. station and sat on a stool. A large puddle of water developed beneath me. I did the radio linkups, and then it was back out into the atrocious conditions, compass in hand once more, as I crossed further moorland and camped at Salters Brook.

By morning most of my equipment was sodden. It was still raining as I continued on over the Howden Moors to the infant River Derwent. The rain eased mid-morning, and it was a magnificent walk down the valley past the reservoirs to Bamford, where a local school was lined up to cheer me on. The Deputy Headmistress gave me tea before doing the final stage of the day's walk via Stanage Edge to Longshaw. No sooner had I set off than the rain descended once more. I reached the lodge soaked. Smiling faintly, I joined the welcoming party, which included the Master Cutler of Sheffield, and walked into the cafe where another wine and cheese party was being held. I didn't stay long before I disappeared to the Warden's room. Here I stripped, and draped all my wet clothes and equipment around the room to dry. I slept on the floor surrounded by the noise of dripping clothes.

The morning brought a fine day, and it was good to feel the warmth of the sun. Ahead of me was a 22-mile walk, Chesterfield for lunch with the Deputy Mayor, and a wine and cheese party in Dronfield in the evening. Sounds a good exercise, this marathon walking, but it was no picnic with such a tight schedule. I slept soundly that night in an orchard.

Having now walked up the western side and most of the northern side of our county, from Dronfield I soon started to walk down the eastern side via Ford, Eckington, Whitwell, Darfoulds, Cresswell Crags, Langwith to Pleasley Vale. At Ford I met Mrs. Betty Lees, the Chairman of North-East Derbyshire, and she walked with me through the Moss Valley to Eckington. She arrived in the official car wearing her walking boots! At Spinkhill 200 schoolchildren lined the street and cheered vigorously. In fact I had originally intended not to use this specific road. One of the National Trust officials caught me just in time, and I had to double-back and walk down the street. I arrived in Pleasley Vale in the early evening and camped, getting my water from a well in a nearby graveyard.

The following morning I had only four miles to walk to Hardwick Hall for lunch. I ambled along and hid in a greenhouse until the appointed hour. The Duchess of Devonshire welcomed me on the steps, and with some thirty dignatories we retired to a small room where a magnificent buffet meal had been prepared. I ate as much as discretion would allow before leaving just after 2 p.m., to walk just over 30 miles to Sandiacre. It was a gruelling walk, simply because I had little time in which to do it. However, by keeping a fast pace and going on the radio programmes from a scrap metal merchant's office, I walked down the Erewash Canal to Sandiacre. Reaching the 'campsite', Gregory's Rose Garden, just after 10 p.m. Sipping their delightful rose-petal wine, I soon forgot about the rigours of the day.

After four hours' sleep, I was once more on the road heading for Melbourne. First halt was Trent Lock to meet the Mayor of Erewash. Then to Shardlow for lunch, before walking beside the Trent and Mersey Canal to Swarkestone. This was very awkward walking, for the tow path is overgrown. So much so that I had to cover my bare legs with overtrousers to avoid being nettled too much. It was a three-hour battle to the bridge. Here I had to avoid the traffic as I crossed the bridge to Kings Newton and into Melbourne.

In the morning I left early with the members of the Melbourne Rotary Club who planned to walk with me to Staunton Harold where a reception had been arranged. The day was my last full one on the walk, as I now began walking round the southern tip of the county. From the delightful setting of Staunton Harold and its beautiful church, I aimed for Smisby. Next were a string of peaceful villages—Netherseal, Clifton Campville, Lullington, Coton on the Elms,—before gaining the River Trent and Burton-on-Trent where I stayed. At Lullington the Landlord of the Inn came out carrying a tea tray. While I made the radio linkups tea was served! This was just one of the many hospitable acts which the escort party and myself experienced. Simply, thank you.

Melbourne Hall.

The following day was Sunday, July 24th, the eleventh and final day of the walk. I took my time, for I always dislike the end of a walk. It had been a personal battle, and with such a heavy social programme one had been stretched both mentally and physically. Added to this, it had been a shared experience with the escort vehicle party. My route was via Rolleston-on-Dove to Tutbury for lunch. We dined in the Dog and Partridge Inn, and the staff came out to welcome us. A little after 1.30 p.m. we left, and I began the last few miles to Sudbury Hall via Scroton. I kept a good pace and reached the outskirts of Sudbury a little before 3 p.m. Having been informed that the crowds were there, I set off not knowing what to expect. Entering the village, the locals came out dressed in costume and began accompanying me. The crowds grew, and a lump came into my throat. I said a formal goodbye and thank you to the back-up team, and walked behind the Ashbourne Town Band. We marched in to the tune of 'Congratulations'. The crowds parted, and near the steps two women in 18th Century costume kissed me and placed garlands of flowers around my neck. By now I was completely disorientated and tried to get away. Someone pointed me in the right direction, and I climbed the steps of the hall to the welcoming party. A bowl of champagne was placed in my hands. Not knowing what I should do with it, I drank the lot and showed it was empty to the assembled crowd. After saying a small and totally unprepared speech, I slipped into the building out of the way.

Later in the afternoon the National Trust escort team of two and myself dined in style in the dining room. I sat in the middle, and the two others were at either end of the table—22 ft. apart! Slowly it began to register that the walk was over. I had walked the boundary in ten and a half days, during which time I had walked 281 miles. The walk had raised a sizeable sum for the Appeal Fund. I was sad that it was over for it had been, for me, a unique walk. It convinced me further that Derbyshire has no equal for scenic quality. Given a couple of spare weeks, I could set off again and leisurely walk the boundary eating chocolate and drinking milk!

Lyme Hall.

My Support Vehicle!

Tutbury Castle.

Dog & Partridge Inn — Tutbury.

PROGRAMME OF DERBYSHIRE BOUNDARY WALK, 1977

(In aid of the National Trust's Derbyshire and Peak District Appeal)

N.B. NATIONAL TRUST properties are in CAPITAL LETTERS

Day	Map No.	Route	Mileage	Total Mileage
1	128/119 O.S. 1:50,000	SUDBURY HALL (10.30 a.m. start)—Oaks Green—Palmer Moor—Doveridge—Dover Bridge—Eatonhall Farm—ROCESTER—Norbury—Church Mayfield—MAPLETON—River Dove—Coldwell Bridge—ILAM. (Arrive 6.30 p.m.)	20	20
2	119	ILAM—DOVEDALE—MILLDALE—WOLFSCOTE DALE—BERESFORD DALE—HARTINGTON—Pilbury—Crowdecote—PAST HIGH WHEELDON—Hollinsclough—Flash—Drystone Edge—Three Shires Head—Cragg Hall.	22	42
3	119	Cragg Hall—Three Shires Head—Cheeks Hill—Can Holes—BUXTON (arrive 11 a.m., leave by 2 p.m.)—Burbage—Wild Moor—Pym Chair—Kettleshulme—Handley Fold Farm—Bow Stones—LYME HALL. (Arrive 6.30 p.m.)	20	62
4	110	LYME HALL—Disley—NEW MILLS—Mellor Moor—Robin's Hood—Picking Rods—Chisworth—Charlesworth—Broadbottom—River Ethrow—Woolley Bridge—TINTWISTLE—Featherbed Moss—Howles Head—Round Hill—Black Hill—Holme Moss T.V.S.—Britland Edge Hill—Withins Edge—Salters Brook Bridge.	24	86
5	110/119	Salters Brook Bridge—Featherbed Moss—HOWDEN MOORS—Outer Edge—Margery Hill—Abbey Brook—Back Tor—Derwent Edge—Bamford—Stanedge Edge—Burbage Valley—LONGSHAW.	24	110
6	119/120	LONGSHAW—WHITEDGE MOOR—Ramsley Moor—Grange Hill—Cutthorpe—CHESTERFIELD (arrive 12 noon)—(leave 2.30 p.m.)—Barlow—Dronfield.	20	130
7	119/120	Dronfield—Troway—FORD—ECKINGTON—Kilamarsh—Whitwell—Steetley Cahpel—Darfoulds—Hall Leys—CRESSWELL CRAGG—Whaley Thorns—Langwith—Shirebrook—Pleasley Vale.	25	155
8	120/129	Pleasley Vale—Pleasley—Newboundmill Farm—HARDWICK HALL—(Arrive 12 noon—leave 2.30 p.m.)—Stanley—Huthwaite—River Erewash—Pinxton—PYE BRIDGE—Ironville—Codnor Park—Stonyford—LANGLEY MILL—River Erewash—Erewash Canal—Trowell—SANDIACRE.	25	180
9	129/128	SANDIACRE—Long Eaton—River Trent—TRENTLOCK—Sawley Cut—SHARDLOW—Trent & Mersey Canal—Swarkestone—Swarkestone Bridge—Kings Newton—MELBOURNE.	21	201
10	128	MELBOURNE—Melbourne Parks—Scotland—STAUNTON HAROLD CHURCH—Wickley Noon—Smisby—Ann Well Place—Blackfordby—Woodville—Noira—Hoodborough Brook—Netherseal—River Mease—Clifton Campuille—Lullington—Coton-on-the-Elms—WALTON-ON-TRENT—River Trent—BURTON-ON-TRENT.	23	224
11	128	BURTON-ON-TRENT—Rolleston-on-Dove—TUTBURY—Scropton—SUDBURY HALL. (Arrive 3.00 p.m.)	12	236

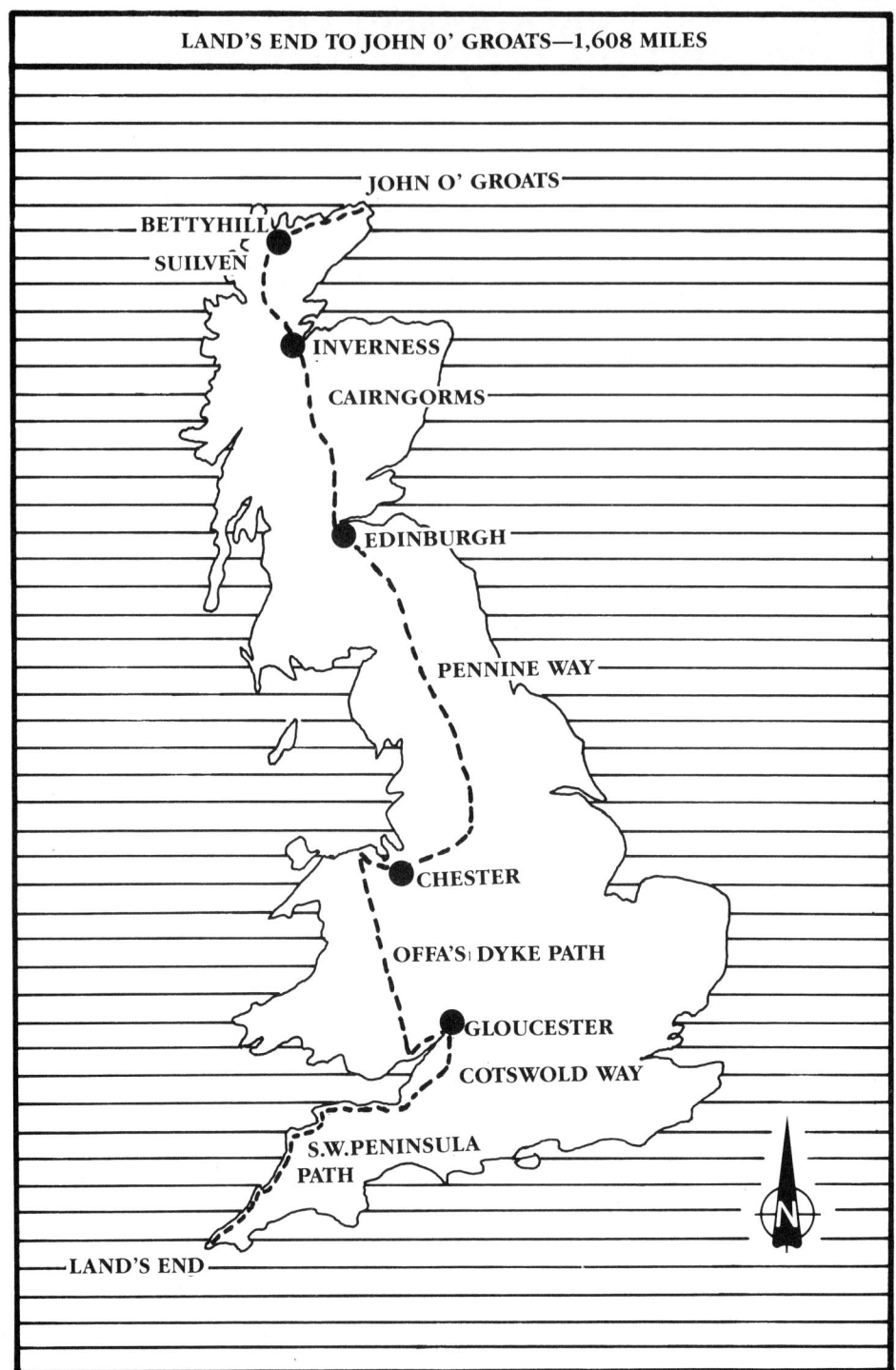

LAND'S END TO JOHN O'GROATS

As part of my training and preparation programme, I knew that before I set off on January 3rd, 1978, to walk the entire coastline of Britain I had to walk the traditional marathon walk, Land's End to John O'Groats. I can safely say that my route was very untraditional, making the walk almost twice as long at 2,587 km. (1,608 miles). My objective was to walk on footpaths as much as possible and see as much of the countryside as I could.

It proved to be a magnificent experience in late summer (July 28 to September 22, 1977). Although much of it was in poor and often atrocious conditions, I found the walk a deeply rewarding experience.

My basic route, which included five long-distance footpaths, went as follows. In walking order: Land's End, North Cornwall Coastal Footpath, North Devon and Somerset Coast Path, Bridgwater, Bath, Cotswold Way, Gloucester, Offa's Dyke Path, Chester, Pennine Way, Lauder, Edinburgh, Forth Bridge, Perth, Cairngorms, Central and North West Highlands, Bettyhill, Thurso, John o' Groats and Duncansby Head.

I left the Sea View Caravan and Camping site near Sennen in Cornwall just after 8 a.m. on July 28 and walked down the road to Land's End. I left early on purpose, so that I could be alone and away from the milling holidaymakers. The task ahead of me weighed on my mind—John o' Groats seemed far away and unreal.

After clicking the camera at the usual sights of the cliffs of Land's End, the hotel, lighthouse, the First and Last House in England and the mileage post which showed John o' Groats 874 miles (1,406 km.) away, I set off along the North Cornwall coast path. It seemed strange to be walking by the sea, seeing cliffs adorned with heather blossom, and above, the hot sun burned down through a cloudless sky. I couldn't really believe my luck at such a perfect start. Little did I know how I was to suffer later!

First & Last House — Land's End.

The first ten days were magical as I walked all the way round the coast to Minehead. I was walking anything up to 32 miles (52 km.) per day with a 50 lb. (23 kg.) rucksack on my back. I didn't like stopping early, feeling that I must use the perfect days to the full. My memory of these days are almost a blurr as I walked past Cape Cornwall, the ruined mines on Botallack Head, picturesque St. Ives, the expanses of golden sands covered with bronzing holidaymakers, Perranporth, St. Isaac, Tintagel, Bude, Hartland Point and onto the stunningly beautiful Clovelly. Instead of retracing my steps and doing a long road walk from here, I walked along the pebbled shore to gain Westward Ho! From Ilfracombe onwards, the scenery changed from the small rugged coves of Cornwall to more dramatic and steeper cliffs. The area around Combe Martin is breathtaking. Sadly I walked through the Valley of Rocks and down to Lynmouth, knowing the final section of the coast lay ahead via Selworthy Beacon to Minehead. Apart from brief skirmishes at either end of Offa's Dyke footpath, it was not until the north Scottish coastline 40 days later that I had the sea for company.

From Minehead I moved inland, passing through the popular tourist haunts of Dunster, Bridgwater, Glastonbury, Wells and on to Bath. I was following little-used rights of way to these places. Everyone I found extremely helpful, and with numerous camp sites in the region I had few problems. This was also a historic pilgrimage—to see the parish church of Bridgwater where the Duke of Monmouth watched from the spire his army's defeat at Sedgemoor in 1685; Glastonbury with its ruined abbey, thorn bush and tor; and Wells Cathedral with its magnificent west front. Bath, too, was admired, especially the Abbey and the nearby Georgian buildings.

From Bath I followed the Cotswold Way to near Cheltenham. While walking the route I met for the first time since leaving Land's End another walker doing a long distance path. He was walking the Cotswold Way north to south from Chipping Campden to Bath.

Since my leaving the coast, the weather had changed and was either overcast or drizzling. But it was good to be in the Cotswolds, walking the western edge of the escarpment with distant views of the River Severn, pleasant woodland and all those beautiful villages, such as Painswick. On my second day in the Cotswolds I walked into Ryeford in the early evening. I asked around if there was anywhere to camp. No one knew anywhere. Eventually the mill owner's wife came to the rescue and offered me the use of her lawn. It is the kindness of such people to a passing traveller that one remembers most after a walk.

Morris Dancers outside Bath Abbey.

Nearing Cheltenham, I turned southwards to Gloucester for a quick look round the Cathedral before walking down the A48 to Chepstow. I dislike road walking, but in some places it is the only way. This was one occasion when thankfully there was a footpath much of the time. Since I would be coming up the whole of Offa's Dyke footpath, I saw little point in walking part of it twice, hence my choice of the road walk. If there is no footpath I always walk on the right hand side and face the oncoming traffic. The large lorries thunder past and pay little heed to a walker. Cars are kinder and generally take a wide berth. To get this section of the walk over as quickly as possible I walked hard, averaging 4-5 miles (5-8 km.) per hour, and after walking 33 miles (53 km.) I reached the camp site close to Sedbury Cliffs, south-east of Chepstow.

I have walked Offa's Dyke before. It is a good route through very varied terrain—from flat countryside to high mountains and moorland. At 168 miles (270 km.) from Chepstow to Prestatyn, it makes a rewarding challenge. Given the bad weather I experienced on it—low cloud and often torrential rain—it was a testing walk.

I had added problems, for I was unwell. I set off from Chepstow without breakfast feeling sick, and had not walked more than a few hundred yards before I was violently sick. For the next six days until I had almost reached Prestatyn in North Wales, I walked along feeling decidedly groggy. All I could put my stomach disorder down to was a tin of peaches I had eaten a day before.

I am very stubborn to say the least. Nothing stands in my way once I start a walk. So instead of seeking medical advice and being better in a day or so, I walked on, and it lasted six days. I ate little, preferring to keep going, my mind active and not dwelling on my poor condition. Despite everything I was still walking well and did 36 miles (58 km.) one day.

I reached Prestatyn at lunchtime, eight days out of Chepstow. I felt no elation with 800 miles (1,287 km.) behind me. The sun came out and the afternoon was as good as a June day, although it was now late August. I collected my next set of maps from the Post Office and strode out along the paths and lanes towards Chester. At Holywell I began seeking a camp site, as I had now walked 29 miles (47 km.) that day. None existed. I walked into the police station to enquire if they knew of a friendly farmer. They didn't, but the receptionist suggested her lawn four miles (6.5 km.) away. I arranged to walk there while she telephoned her husband to expect a bearded stranger. She also added that he should make sure there was hot water for a bath and that there were a couple of pork chops in the fridge. It was a delightful twist to the day's events—after my feeling low in morale—to find such genuine generosity.

Dufton — on Pennine Way. N. Half.

The next day I was in Chester stocking up with food and films ready for the Pennine Way. I was now feeling my usual buoyant self and strode out, walking 38 miles (61 km.) into Macclesfield. I was soaked and tired, and finding a bed and breakfast house I slept soundly. The following day I walked into the Peak District, doing 25 miles (40 km.), which meant that in 30 hours I had walked 63 miles (101 km.). I camped at Edale ready for the Pennine Way next day. There was no need to push myself so hard on this walk, but by Edale I was already four days ahead of my schedule. The following morning brought heavy rain and low cloud. I set off up the Pennine Way, the third time in 12 months! I had hoped to walk it in ten days, but the weather was atrocious. The crossing of the Cheviot Hills was in some of the worst weather I have ever experienced. Soaked to the skin, with horizontal rain and gale force winds, I began to imagine that the elements simply toyed with me. I walked into Kirk Yetholm after completing the walk in 11 days.

Up to this point in the walk from Land's End, now some 1,200 miles (1,931 km.) behind me, I had been to all the places before. Ahead was new ground, and as I descended from The Schil towards Kirk Yetholm I yelled with delight—Scotland here I come!

First of all I made my way through the Border country to Kelso and on to Lauder and Dalkeith. As always when in Edinburgh, I camped at the Little France site, on this occasion finding the driest patch available! Next morning I walked into Edinburgh. The sun shone as I walked over the Royal Mile and down to Princes Street. I lingered awhile absorbing the scene, but the noise and crowds soon became a nuisance and I slipped away. It surprised me how soon I was out of the city as I aimed for the Forth Road Bridge. I crossed the bridge using the pedestrian lane, and it was almost uncanny walking across so much water. The bridge itself remains a superlative monument of engineering.

From the bridge I continued on through more gentle rolling countryside to Dunfermline and Kinross, with Loch Leven on its eastern side where Mary Queen of Scots was imprisoned. Next I crossed the Ochil Hills to Perth, in the now familiar unkind weather. Perth was a major point of the walk, for I now left the lanes behind and entered the unforgettable world of high mountains, deep glens with deer and buzzards and rushing torrents of rivers. First I walked through Glen Shee, before following the line of General Wade's Military Road to Aberfeldy, where I camped. Next day I was back in the mountains as I crossed to Pitlochry and moved onto the Killiecrankie Pass and Blair Atholl.

Suilven and Lochinver.

Now I was in magnificent countryside, and the next two weeks I spent camping wild, seeing few people. Often during a 24-hour period I would see no-one, and shops would be 60 miles (97 km.) apart. Carrying a heavy rucksack with four days' dehydrated food with me all the time, I began the crossing of the Cairngorms. Bad weather meant that I kept to the glens rather than ascending the mountains. There seemed little point going by compass all the time and having no view. Better to keep low, enjoy the remote scenery and observe the wildlife. My route was basically Glen Tilt, Glen Dee and the Lairig Ghru and on to Boat of Garten. Further mountain crossings brought me four days later to Inverness. I walked into the town in the early evening with the sun enriching the colours of the neighbouring hills and the blue sea of the Moray Firth.

While the Cairngorms had been memorable, the next few days from Inverness were by far the finest of all. I walked through glen after glen, disturbing red deer as I went. Buzzards were numerous, and on several occasions eagles soared high above. I was now heading more into the hills of the north-western corner of Sutherland. The mountains were still submerged in cloud, and rain streamed down, but I did not worry. What I could see of the landscape was captivating and of a superlative nature. Then, quite dramatically, when almost in the final range of mountains, the weather changed. Gone were the miserable conditions. In their place came blue sky, hot sun and the russet colours of autumn. The clarity was astonishing, and I have never had better conditions here, even in June.

I climbed a mountain, and as I gained the summit a sight to create joy in a mountaineer's heart met my eyes. Ahead were these noble and unforgettable mountains of north-west Scotland—Cul Mor, Suilven and Canisp. I stared long and hard at their beauty. Such a fine reward for experiencing so much bad weather was all the more appreciated.

Two days later I reached Lairg and stocked up with food. My final mountains before the north coast of Scotland lay ahead. First I headed into Ben Armine Forest, bound for Ben Kilbreck. I didn't get far before being turned back! I suppose I had been lucky to have come this far without meeting any deer-stalking parties. It is the first time I have ever been turned back, but really there was no alternative unless one wanted to be bloody-minded. So instead of ascending these noble mountains I had to do a long detour around their bases to Bettyhill. I was now six days ahead of my 64-day schedule, and was not going to lose this lead, so I had no option but to walk hard. In the final eight days to John o' Groats, I covered 252 miles (406 km.)—an average of 31 and a half miles (50 km.) per day.

From Bettyhill I kept to the coast, past Dounreay Atomic Experimental Station, and so came into Thurso. Now with a slightly slower pace, for I hate the end of a major walk, I continued on to Dunnet Bay, John o' Groats, and Duncansby Head, the most north-eastern point of Britain. There was no joy in my heart. I had done what I had set out to do and in only 57 days (28 and a quarter miles, or 45.5. km., per day), ending up seven days ahead of my schedule. I hadn't set off from Land's End with the intention of walking so hard, but to the last person I had seen at home before I boarded the train to Penzance to start the trip, I had said I would be a week ahead at the finish!

John O'Groats Hotel.

Duncansby Rock Stacks.

LAND'S END TO JOHN O'GROATS WALK 1977

Day	Map 1:50,000 O.S. Sheet No.	Route	Mileage	Overall Mileage
1	203	Land's End—Cornwall North Coast Path—Whitesand Bay—Cape Cornwall—Gurnard's Head—Zennor Head—St. Ives.	20	20
2	203	St. Ives—Lelant—Hayle—Godrevy Point—Navax Point—Portreath.	19	39
3	203 & 200	Portreath—Porthowan—St. Agnes Head—Perranporth—Penhale Point—Crantock—Newquay.	20	59
4	200	Newquay—Watergate Bay—Park Head—Trevose Head—Trevone—Stepper Point—Padstow.	18	77
5	200	Padstow—Ferry—Daymer Bay—Polzeath—Kellan Head—Port Isaac—Tregardock Beach—Tintagel.	20	97
6	200 & 190	Tintagel—Boscastle—Crackington—Haven—Dizzard Point—Widemouth Sand—Bude.	22	119
7	190	Bude—Steeple Point—Marsland Mouth—Speke's Mill Mouth—Hartland Point.	20	139
8	190	Hartland Point—Beckland Bay—Clovelly—Peppercombe—Babbacombe Mouth—Westward Ho.	21	160
9	180	Westward Ho—Appledore—Ferry—Inston—Bickleton—Barnstaple—Upcott—Braunton—Saunton—Croyde Bay.	20	180
10	180	Croyde Bay—Woolacombe Sand—Bull Point—Ilfracombe—Widmouth Head—Combe Martin—Elwill Bay.	24	204
11	180 & 181	Elwill Bay—Woody Bay—Lynmouth—Foreland Point—Culbone—Porlock Bay.	23	227
12	181	Porlock Bay—Minehead—Dunster Beach—Blue Anchor—Watchet.	20	247
13	181 & 182	Watchet—Doniford—West Quantoxhead—Quantock Hills—Merridge Hill—Timbercombe—Enmore—Durleigh—Bridgewater.	26	273
14	182	Bridgewater—Knowle—Woolavington—River Bridge—Blackford—Middle Stoughton—Clewer—Cheddar.	22	295
15	182 & 172	Cheddar—Gorge—Charterhouse—Ubley—Chew Stoke—Chew Magna—Publow—Compton Dando.	23	318
16	172	Compton Dando—Burnett—Corston—Bath—Cotswold Way—Lansdown Hill—Cold Ashton.	21	339
17	172 & 162	Cold Ashton—Dyrham—Dodington Park—Little Sodbury—Kilcutt—Wooton under Edge.	25	364
18	162	Wooton under Edge—North Nibley—Dursley—Nympsfield—Standish Park—Painswick.	26	390

19	162	Painswick—Painswick Hill—Upton St. Leonards—Gloucester—Alney Island—Minsterworth—Northwood Green—Littledean.	22	412
20	162	Littledean—Forest of Dean—Upper Soudley—Yorkley—Bream—St. Briavels, Sedbury (Chepstow)	23	435
21	162	Sedbury—Offa's Dyke Path—Tintern—Lower Redbrook—Kymin—Monmouth.	20	455
22	162 & 161	Monmouth—Dingeston—Llantilio Crossenny—White Castle—Llangathock Lingoed—Pandy—Trewyn.	20	475
23	161 & 148	Trewyn—Hay Bluff—Hay on Wye—Newchurch.	20	495
24	148 & 137	Newchurch—Gladestrey—Kington—Evenjobb—Whitton—Knighton.	23	518
25	137	Knighton—Llanfair Hill—Lower Spead—Churchtown—Montgomery.	21	539
26	137 & 126	Montgomery—Forden—Buttington—River Severn—Four Cro—Llanymynech.	22	561
27	126 & 117 & 116	Llanymynech—Trefowen—Old Race Course—Craignant—Chirk Castle—Llandegla.	23	584
28	116	Llandegla—Moel Gyw—Moel Fammau—Moel Arthur—Bodfari—Rhuallt—Trelawnyd—Gwaenysgor—Prestatyn.	26	610
29	116 & 117	Prestatyn—Gyrn Castle—Trelogan—Whitford—Holywell—Halkyn—Flint—Northop—Hawarden—Chester.	23	633
30	117 & 118	Chester—Christleton—Duddon—Cotebrook—Little Budworth—Winsford—Middlewich—River Dane.	21	654
31	118	River Dane—Cranage—Twemlow Green—Withington—Siddington—Macclesfield—Rainow.	22	676
32	118 & 119 & 110	Rainow—Jenkin Chapel—Goyt Valley—Burbage—Buxton—Peak Dale—Peak Forest—Old Moor—Mam Tor—Edale.	22	698
33	110	Edale—Pennine Way—Kinder—Bleaklow—Crowden—Great Crowden Brook.	21	719
34	110 & 104	Great Crowden Brook—Black Hill—M62—Millstone Edge—White Horse Inn.	20	739
35	104	White Horse Inn—Warland Reservoir—Stoodley Pike—Colden—Ponden—Lothersdale.	26	765
36	99	Lothersdale—Gargrave—Malham—Fountains Fell.	25	790
37	99	Fountains Fell—Lenyghent—Horton—Cam End—Gayle—Great Shunner Fell.	28	818
38	92	Great Shunner Fell—Thwaite—Keld—Tan Hill Inn—Baldersdale.	24	842
39	92	Baldersdale—Middleton in Teesdale—Cauldron Snout—High Cup—Dufton.	27	869
40	87	Dufton—Knock Fell—Crols Fell—Garrigill—Alston—Slaggyford.	25	894
41	87	Slaggyford—Thirlwall Castle—Hadrian's Wall—Wark Forest.	25	919
42	87	Wark Forest—Bellingham—Brownrigg—Head—Redesdale Forest.	20	939
43	80	Redesdale Forest—Bryness—Glew Green—Russell Cairn—Windy Gyle.	20	959

44	80	Windy Gyle—The Schil—The Cheviot—Burnhead—Kirk Yetholm.	10	969
45	74	Kirk Yetholm—B6352—Kelso—Smailholm—Covehouse—Loanend Covert.	22	991
46	74 & 73 & 66	Loanend Covert—Legerwood—Lauder—Inchkeith Hill—Oxton—Clints Hill.	24	1,015
47	66	Clints Hill—Middleton—Gorebridge—Loanhead—Gilmerton—Little France Campsite.	20	1,035
48	66 & 65	Little France Campsite—Edinburgh—Braepark—Queensferry—Blackness—Bo'ness—Grangemouth—Kincardine.	25	1,060
49	65 & 68	Kincardine—Kilbagie—Forest Hill—Dollar—Glenquey Reservoir—Glendevon—Borland Glen—Tonquey Fauls—Water of May.	21	1,081
50	58	Water of May—Pathstruie—Forgandenny—Bridge of Earn—Perth.	22	1,103
51	58 & 52	Perth—Luncarty—Shocie Burn—Glen Shee—Ballachraggon—General Wades Military Road—Glen Cochill.	23	1,126
52	52 & 43	Glen Cochill—Loch Kennard—Little Ballinluig—Pitlochry—Garry Bridge—Blair Atholl.	22	1,148
53	43	Blair Atholl—Glen Tilt—Falls of Tarf—White Bridge.	21	1,169
54	43 & 36	White Bridge—Glen Dee—Lairig Ghru—Loch Morlich.	24	1,193
55	36 & 27	Loch Morlich—Boat of Garten—Carrbridge—Creag-n-h-Lolaire—Strathdearn.	23	1,216
56	27 & 26	Strathdearn—General Wade's Military Road—Inverness—Mains of Bunchrew.	20	1,236
57	26	Mains of Bunchrew—Kirkhall—Beauly—Urray Forest—Marybank—Contin.	21	1,257
58	26 & 20	Contin—Falls of Rogie—Loch Garve—Little Garve—Aultguish Inn—Strath Vaich—Loch Vaich—Gleann Mor.	24	1,281
59	20 & 16	Gleann Mor—Alladale Lodge—Croick—Starth Cuileannach—Amat—Oykel—Invercassley.	21	1,302
60	16	Invercassley—Lairg—Dalchork Wood—Dalnessie.	20	1,322
61	16	Dalnessie—An Crom Allt—Loch Choire—Corriefeuran Hill—Loch Naver.	20	1,342
62	16 & 10	Loch Naver—Naver Forest—Inchlampie—Meall Bad Na Cuaiche—Loch Strathy—Strathy Forest.	20	1,362
63	10 & 11	Strathy Forest—Strathy—Melvich—Reay—Scrabster—Westfield—Thurso.	22	1,384
64	11 & 12	Thurso—Castletown—Dunnet Bay—Dunnet Head—Scarfskerry—East May—Gills—Huna—John o' Groats.	28	1,412

NOTE: My pedometer recorded 1,608 miles for the walk, and, as the above schedule was made with a map measurer, I think the pedometer reading is the true overall mileage.

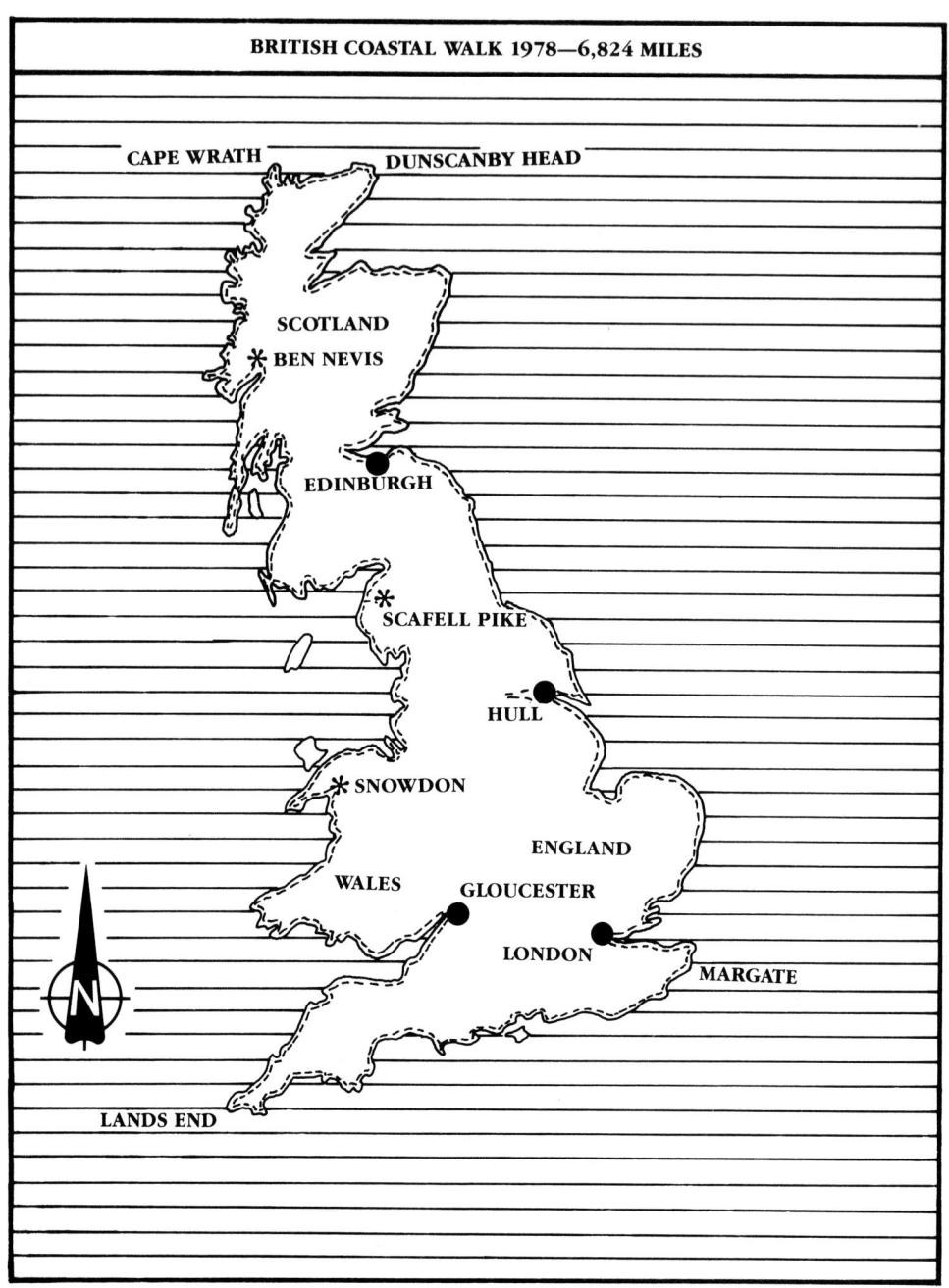

COASTAL REFLECTIONS

THE ROUTE:
I planned the route clockwise from London for two reasons. Firstly I am superstitious, and to walk anti-clockwise—the Devil's way—was unacceptable. Secondly, I would be tackling the west coast from south to north, the best way; psychologically it is better to appear to be going uphill than downhill. As a result I had to keep a tight grip on my mind when I turned right at John o' Groats and headed downhill to London!

Apart from a few bombing ranges and industrial complexes, I walked along the cliff top or shore all the way. No ferries—I walked up the estuaries and used the first road bridge. This involved huge distances inland. Take, for example, the River Humber. On reaching Spurn Head, I could see Grimsby and Cleethorpes four miles away. To get there via the Boothferry Bridge, Isle of Axeholme and Scunthorpe required a walk of 140 miles! The total length of the coastline of Britain—England, Wales and Scotland—is 6,180 miles. Using my rules I walked just short of 6,900 miles.

HIGHLIGHTS:
So much happened on the walk—weather, scenery, wild life, human performance and interesting people met—that it is impossible to do adequate justice to them all. Yet a few highlights will remain with me always. I reached Land's End in early February with 1,100 miles behind me. Another aspect of my planning was to set off at the start of a new year, after the shortest day, and do the south west corner first—the mildest part of Britain, statistically—in January and February. It was, therefore, a surprise and delight to walk along the snow-covered sands of Sennen Cove. Westwards lay the Scilly Isles, covered in snow for the first time in 30 years.

Four days later, in North Cornwall near Boscastle, I was caught in the worst blizzards for 30 years. I spent eight days camping and walking in 25 feet snowdrifts. The scenes were incredible—huge cornices on cliff tops, kicking steps up 400 feet snow slopes with no axe, stiles lost and submerged by the drifts, and crossing roads from hedge to hedge and looking down onto the road signs. Helicopters thrashed through the air rescuing stranded coastguards. Milk lorries were only able to negotiate main roads, and farmers used all their ingenuity to get to them. Finally, I walked into Lynmouth after eight days, the first person to reach the cut-off coastal village. The shop shelves were bare, and I was unable to buy any chocolate!

Dunrottor Castle — East Coast of Scotland.

John Merrill and coastal equipment.

Staithes — Yorkshire Coast.

From Barrow-on-Furness I crossed the sands of Duddon Bay. I was accompanied for the 14-mile walk by an insurance agent in a suit and slip-on shoes. On reaching any mud, he ran across leaving his shoes embedded! At a deep river channel he took off his shoes and socks, rolled up his trousers and waded up to his knees in the cold water. Halfway across I made him pose for a photograph. On gaining the other bank I promised to send him a copy. With aplomb, he gave me his business card! Later in the day I learnt he drove a Rolls Royce.

As I made my way round Loch Hourn, north of Mallaig, I had been six days without a shop and three days without seeing anyone. I had one dehydrated meal left, and a a few bars of Dextrosol—enough to survive. I passed a croft and was spotted. The owner had heard me on Radio Scotland from Ardnamurchan Lighthouse, and had worked out when I would pass. She jumped into a boat and caught up with me on the seaweed-clad shore. We sat on the rocks and ate cheese sandwiches. Before leaving she presented me with a 2 lb. Christmas cake; the date was August 10th! I ate half of it that evening, more for breakfast, and by lunchtime next day it was gone!

I have had to keep a very tight grip on my emotions, and even now I will not release them. The only time I really registered what I had done was as I neared Southend-on-Sea, my last point on the coast. It was dark, but as I approached the sea front from Shoeburyness I could look across the Thames for the first time and see the lights on the Isle of Grain and Gravesend. I stood a long while in silence and soaked up the scene.

On the natural history side, I shall never forget following Spring—seeing violets, celandine and primula from early February to June, and shelducks almost daily for five months. A mute swan with twelve cygnets, an eagle's eyrie, stags fighting, stroking red deer fawns, watching otters, red squirrels running across my rucksack, and seeing the elusive pine marten. Above all, the experience of watching a year blossom, fade and die, as I walked through the four seasons.

FAVOURITE PLACES:
Almost impossible to state, for so much of our coastline is breathtaking, even in industrial areas. Cornwall, Dorset and Devon are very good. Pembrokeshire is still outstanding—I have walked it four times, and its beauty and character does not lessen, it heightens. The Solway coast is unknown and unspoilt. The west coast of Scotland has no equal, it is all very, very good. Caithness is full of surprises and exceptionally beautiful; so too is Fife; Northumberland is excellent; and the Yorkshire coast is always a joy to walk down. Norfolk was a delightful surprise, and some of its beaches are the best anywhere.

EQUIPMENT:
I spent 170 nights under canvas, using the same tent throughout, made specially for me by Blacks of Greenock. I had intended to camp out more, but the poor weather simply dictated otherwise. Although the material has faded and the rubber rings are starting to perish, there is no other sign of wear and not once did it leak or let me down. Even in Force 9 gales it remained stable. I used four different Blacks sleeping bags—Icelandic Mummy for winter, Tromso for spring, Backpacker for summer and Highland 68 for autumn. They were all perfect for the job, and the Backpacker, with only 12 oz. of goosedown, was beautifully warm and adequate for summer use.

For January and February I wore climbing breeches with my calves bare. From the beginning of March onwards I wore shorts—one pair only—right through to now (I am still wearing them!). I carried only two cotton shirts. The thicker one I wore until early May, and the lighter one for the next five months. Neither was ever washed! I used the same Norwegian pullover throughout. With the constant rubbing of my two cameras and binoculars, several large holes have developed. My socks were Norwegian ragg type, using a short and long pair together. Approximately three weeks' use, without washing, was all I allowed them, by which time they were extremely thin on the heels. I wore out 33 pairs! Throughout the walk I walked in Berghaus Scarpa Monte Rosa boots. I carried no other footwear with me. Normally I allow 2,500 miles per pair, but I decided to wear the first pair out. They did 3,800 miles! The other two pairs I used both did 2,500 miles. I had no blisters, which I believe is because each pair of boots had done 500 miles before I used them on the walk, and were, therefore, well broken in. Also, of course, they are a very rugged and comfortable boot.

Until the end of April, I carried and used a Blacks Snowgoose Duvet. Very warm, and well worth the extra weight in the rucksack. My anorak throughout was a Blacks Highland jacket —ventile outer, cotton inner. Apart from general wear from constant use, it had proved itself to be a very dependable item of equipment. My raingear was a Blacks Grampian cagoule—very serviceable but, like them all, caused condensation inside. I had two sets of Berghaus Gore-tex Mistral jackets, overtrousers and gaiters. I am not sold on the special properties of Gore-tex, and it is something I would like to test further. Perhaps I gave the jackets an unfair test because I was unable to wash them. As on my last three walks, my rucksack was a Berghaus Cyclops Serac. It has been carried for 8,500 miles in the last 15 months. Apart from some of the straps fraying, it remains in excellent order and a pleasure to carry, although one never completely gets used to carrying 50/60 lbs. daily.

FOOD:
For cooking, I used a Trangia stove until the end of April. I found it worked perfectly, the only drawback being that the methylated spirits blackened the pans. From May onwards I used a Camping Gaz Globetrotter stove. Reliable, just right for one person, and very compact. I thought the two one-pint pans might be too small, but I soon adjusted and found them to be all that I needed. Half my food was dehydrated, supplied by Raven Foods. I had seven different main meals from their Standard and Regal ranges. I also had their three instant desserts. Despite going 6-8 days on this food at one time, I never tired of eating it or found my performance reduced. I ate plenty of Alpen for breakfast, and tinned or fresh food when able to find a shop. During the day I ate chocolate—6/8 bars per day. The grand total for the walk—1,511! Usually I drank two pints of milk a day—consuming 528 altogether! Most of the time I weighed 4-6 lbs. more than when I set off. Only in the closing stages, when the strain and cumulative effect began to bite, did I actually lose weight, ending up 9 lbs. lighter.

PHYSICAL ACHIEVEMENT:
Prior to this walk, I had walked up to 2,000 miles without a rest day. I felt ready, mentally and physically, to tackle this one. Apart from walking 4,000 miles the previous year in preparation—which included the Pennine Way three times and a 1,600-mile Land's End—John o' Groats walk— I could not think of any way to prepare. It was simply a matter of getting off and getting to grips with the problem and sorting out everything on the ground. I believe the mental and physical approach was right.

On reaching the Firth of Clyde, I had 3,300 miles behind me, walked in 126 days—an average of 28 miles per day. My right foot was increasingly painful. At first I shrugged it off, thinking it to be a physical barrier I had to pass through. The pain grew worse, and at Greenock Royal Infirmary the specialist diagnosed a 'fatigue fracture' on my fourth metatarsal. I had pushed the human body to the limit. Apparently, by using my feet at such a high level performance (they have the most complex bone structure of the human body) my bones had become brittle. There was nothing I could do about it; the bone simply snapped through use. I had not tripped up or anything. It was a stunning blow, and I had created medical history.

I spent a month living in plaster up to my knee, totally immobilised. A one and a half mile walk took me two and a half hours. To have ignored the doctor's advice and carried on would have resulted in serious and possibly permanent damage. To return home would have been defeat. What had happened was not defeat but a story of the walk. After a month the plaster was removed and the bone had healed.

I was told to have two weeks' walking around the garden. I had 24 hours' rest and then climbed a 1,500 foot mountain, a 2,000 foot one the following day and, six days out of plaster, I ascended Ben Lomond, over 3,000 feet. The next day I told the doctors I was off the following morning! I knew mentally I had to set off or the walk would be over.

In front of me was the hardest part of the walk—the west coast of Scotland. I could only manage 15—17 miles a day. I limped for six weeks and was in considerable pain. This I find very interesting—that one can pick oneself up after a month's lay-off, totally unfit and having put on one and a half stones in weight, and still cope with tremendous physical and mental problems. In effect, and against many doctors' advice, I walked myself back to fitness.

On reflection, my performance can be charted very easily. It was not until I had reached 2,000 miles that I reached my peak. I held it for 500 miles before it declined at 3,000 miles and the effort became harder and harder. From the time of the fracture I walked 3,600 miles without a rest day. Again it is a similar chart, but took a longer period of time because of my limp. I was very tired physically and mentally at the end, but have no doubts that I could have continued. The one figure which does seem very important is 200 miles per week. All runners who have tried to do 200 or more miles a week have had stress fractures in the leg. I was walking 200-230 miles every week, and as much as 40 miles in one day. In terms of actual walking days I planned on a 256-day schedule. Despite the fracture, I did in in 257!

Cames Head — Pembrokeshire.

Beach near Ullapool.

Chain Path — Nr. Kirkcaldy.

WALK'S ACHIEVEMENTS:
While the walk itself was my prime motivation—I did it simply because I wanted to—it has created many records. Obviously, the first person to walk the entire coastline of Britain. The first person to do the longest possible walk from Land's End to John o' Groats—a walk of just over 3,800 miles. I also took the longest walk between Snowdon, Scafell Pike and Ben Nevis—some 1,200 miles. The list is endless when one starts saying, the first person to walk all the promenades in one year, etc...

While I did the walk I allowed it to be used to raise money for the Royal Commonwealth Society for the Blind. By allowing people to be sponsored to walk with me for 5 miles, or hold a lottery or raffle on the time I reached a specific point on the coastline, the walk raised £40,000. The money was used for sight restoration operations in India. Approximately 13,000 people had their sight restored by cataract operation as a result of the walk.

CONCLUSIONS:
Do I have any regrets? None—the walk was an experience of a lifetime. I only wished I could have had a swim in the sea—the water was too cold! Would I do it again? No, not that I don't want to, but the memories of the first one would be shattered.

What next? Within 24 hours of reaching London, I was avidly reading a guide to a walk around Mont Blanc. I planned to do this the following summer. Before that I hoped to be in America, walking the 2,000-mile Appalachian Trail, in preparation for a much tougher walk in that country.

Finally, a walk of this size relies on the spontaneous help given by so many people. So I will end by simply saying 'thank you' to everyone I met on the way—the general public, civic officials, police and coastguards. For the moment, I realise I can get into a car, ride on a bus or train, and wear long trousers and normal shoes! I am sorry it is all over.

Approaching Snowdon.

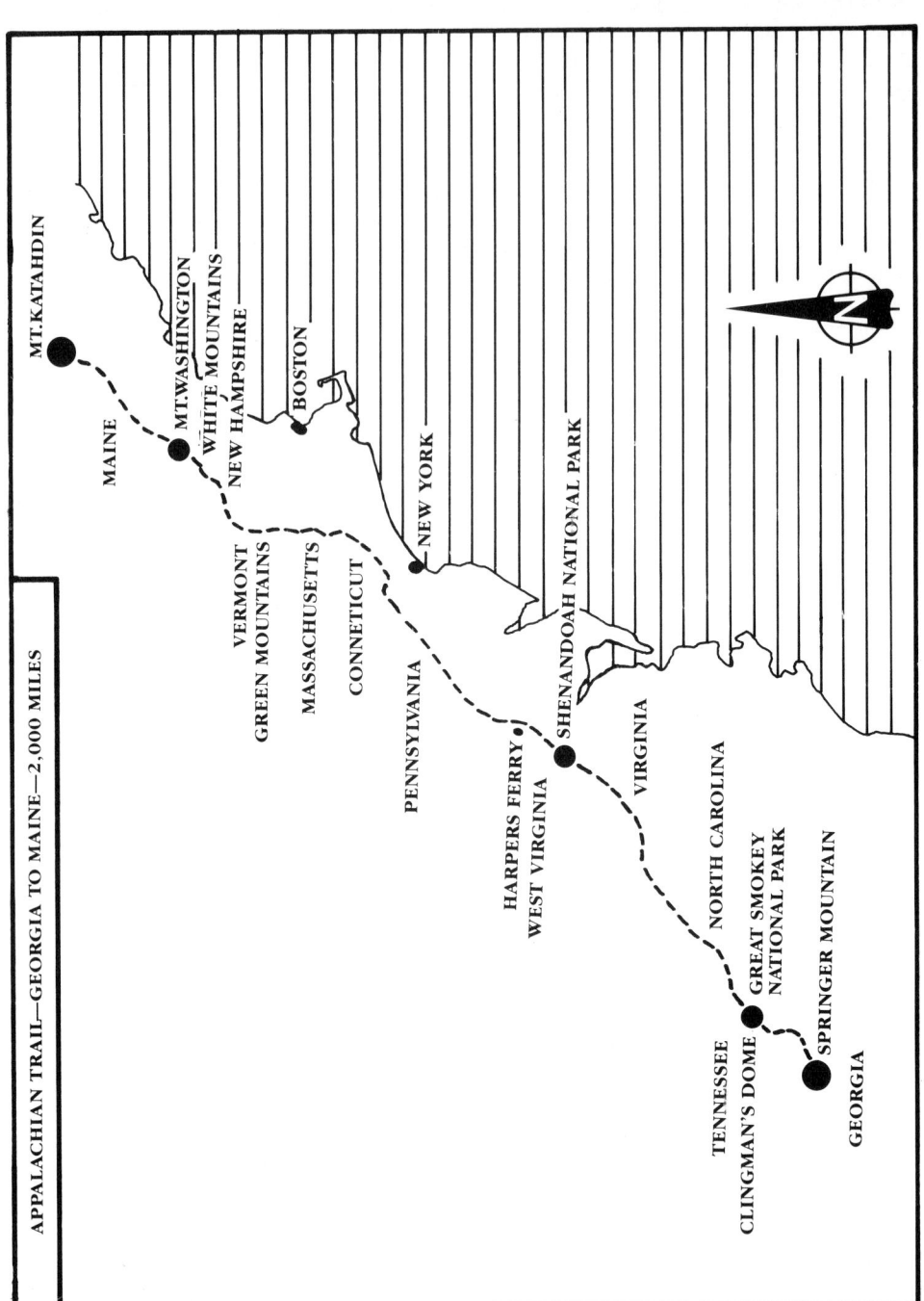

FOLLOW THE WHITE BLAZE

For five days I had been walking through dense forest, seeing no one, only hearing the startled chirp of a chipmunk as he fled from my approach, or a flurry of leaves as a ground hog ran away. I was at peace with the world, shouldering a 50 pound load and enjoying the rigours of American wilderness. My eyes were constantly alert, for although I followed a 6″ × 2″ white blaze on the tree trunks, I still had to ensure that I was walking the right way. To lose the trail could be fatal. I also had to watch where I was putting my feet. Snakes abound, and America's two most lethal—the rattlesnake and copperhead—were frequently seen.

The idea of a continuous footpath through the Appalachian Mountains, the oldest mountain range in the world, on the eastern side of America, came from Forester and City Planner Benton MacKaye, in the early 1920s.

In 1926 the job of cutting a trail through the forests and along the ridges had begun. By 1937 it was complete, and today still basically follows the original line through fourteen eastern states. The trail keeps to the highest ground all the time. However, 90% is through forests with no views, which to an Englishman is very frustrating.

Before setting off I was in contact with the Appalachian Trail Conference at Harpers Ferry in Virginia—the organising body of the Trail, and from whom I purchased the ten guide books and forty maps which cover the whole trail. Walking in the wilderness means you have to be self-sufficient. On much of the trail there is a wooden shelter, three-sided, every seven miles, where you can camp, light a fire, and get water. I set off with eight days' food, tent, sleeping bag, stove and rain gear. To get further provisions I had to leave the trail and find a store. To each of six Post Offices near the trail I sent seven days' dehydrated food, which ensured I would not starve and would not have to carry too much. The guides advised setting off in early April to follow Spring north. The vast majority of people who attempt the trail walk south to north. The trail is hard, very lonely, and passes through very tough countryside. In 1978, 1,500 attempted to walk the whole distance but only 41 actually made it.

Appalachian Trail sign.

In the first three weeks I passed 400 people attempting the walk. I had allowed three months, which in theory was ample time as I generally average 28 miles per day. Unfortunately the trail has been relocated in many places—information which is not in the guides or maps. I ran out of time and had to miss out 150 miles of trail.

Leaving the summit Springer Mountain on April 6th 1979, the trees were not in leaf. For seven days I walked along ridges between 4,000 and 5,000 feet. On the eighth day I dropped to the valley floor. It was a remarkable experience, for, as I descended to 1,500 feet, I suddenly noticed the trees coming into leaf and spring flowers emerging from the ground. I turned a corner, stopped in my tracks, and gazed at the first house I had seen for seven days.

The Great Smoky Mountains are a dramatic change, and brought me into contact with black bears. As I entered the park I had to obtain my backpacker's permit to 'thru hike' in a given time. I was also informed I must sleep in the shelters, which have a bear-proof grid across the front. I never saw any, thank goodness. It was too early; they were still hibernating. 500 miles later, while crossing the only other National Park on the trail, the Shenandoah, I camped at Big Meadows campground. Here half the campers were up all night keeping the bears away. My most alarming experience with a bear came midway between the Smokies and Shenandoah. I camped at about 4,800 feet on Sugar Run Mountain, near Pearisburg, Virginia. At 10.30 p.m. I was rudely awoken by a growling bear trying to get into the tent! I banged my pans for all I was worth and managed to frighten him away. I couldn't sleep then. Around 2.15 a.m. he came again, more determined. Again by banging my pans and blowing my whistle, he eventually ran off. This time I had had enough. There was a locked shed belonging to a closed campground nearby. Finding the door open I quickly took the tent down and spent the rest of the night there.

The mountains in the Shenandoah National Park, although quite high, are not nearly as steep as those further south on the Trail. Once out of the park, the mountains recede in height to about 1,800 feet. It isn't until Massachusetts that they begin to grow again, reaching 6,200 feet in the white mountains of New Hampshire. In New York State, where I crossed the Hudson River, I reached the lowest point of the trail, 130 feet above sea level.

The White Mountains are very impressive above timberline, but can be very dangerous. Signposts warn of the hazards of exposure and being a place for fit people only. Many have died from exposure, and on Mount Washington it can snow at any time of the year. Fortunately I had a clear, warm June day when I climbed the mountain. The meteorological station on top bears a plaque recording that in 1934 the world's highest wind speed was recorded here—231 miles per hour!

Once across the White Mountains, I began entering the final stages of the walk through the State of Maine. Much of it is around the 2,000 feet mark, and the trail passes numerous lakes. Unfortunately I was walking in the blackfly season. In New York State I had experienced clouds of mosquitoes, and never before have my legs and arms been so badly bitten. The blackflies were even worse, and I was frequently running to shake them off. But the joy of this area is to see Baxter Peak, just over 5,200 feet.

It is a very imposing mountain and dominates the whole area. This is the mountain you have striven for weeks to reach. I ambled slowly along a river, where I had a swim, before entering the Baxter State Park. The regulations were off-putting, for if all the camp sites are full you cannot enter. Nor can you begin your ascent of Baxter Peak after midday.

I camped at Katahdin Stream campground, and the following day, in absolutely perfect weather, I began the climb. Three hours later I was standing at the northern terminus of the Appalachian Trail. The view was extensive, but before beginning my descent I climbed along the Knife Edge ridge. This is not part of the trail, but is a superb ridge scramble, like our own Crib Goch route in Snowdonia. Sadly I left the summit. The following day, in pouring rain, I began making my way back to New York and home.

Apart from trouble with bears, snakes were a constant threat. Most people carry a snake bite kit, a razor blade and suction cap. I didn't, for the thought of having to cut and suck the venom out did not appeal. I saw nine different snakes, including rat snakes, corn snakes, chicken snakes and garter snakes. These are basically 'safe'. The poisonous timber rattlesnake and the copperheads were the ones to avoid. I saw several sunning themselves on the trail. Rather than walk over them I would throw a stone or branch at them and make them move. One of my finest sights was an eight foot long black eastern diamond rattlesnake. Its body in the centre was a thick as a man's arm.

Another very real danger was thunderstorms. The ones we get in Britain are tame by comparison. In one week I experienced eight ferocious storms. On one occasion I could hear thunder behind me and began to run in an attempt to reach a shelter six miles away. It was a hopeless task, and within twenty minutes I was in the middle of the storm on the crest of a 4,000 foot ridge. Lightning came down close to me. Hurriedly I took off pack, cameras and watch, and left them by a tree 100 feet away. I waited ten minutes as the lightning flickered around me, then I couldn't stand it any longer. I simply grabbed my rucksack and ran down the ridge through dense foliage. I reached the shelter two hours later. That night another storm blew up and lasted three hours. Four days later I was in another equally violent storm and was pelted by three quarters of an inch diameter hailstones.

One 'danger' which I hadn't expected on the trail was drugs. Yet in many places other walkers offered me hash, marijuana or even acid. Naturally I refused, but it made you uncomfortable when they were staying in the shelter with you. Equally alarming were reports of mugging, rape and robbery on the trail. In one shelter a notice advised walkers that the next twelve miles were dangerous: 'Just keep going and don't talk to anyone.'

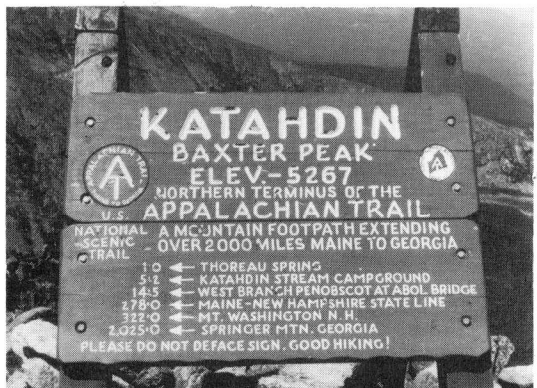

Appalachian Trail notice board in the summit of Baxter Peak, Katahdin, Maine.

Knife Edge Ridge — Mt. Katahdin.

John Merrill on Mt. Katahdin.

Being my first visit to the States, I had to get used to their way of life. At first it was very strange, and I couldn't grasp what was happening, nor their dependence on the motor car. But as the weeks passed I slipped into their way of living and enjoyed it. I got used to staying in motels, having ice with everything and going to the restaurant or diner for a meal. I sampled all their current eating houses—Macdonalds, Dunkin' Donuts, Wendy's, Burger King, Pizza Hut and Kentucky Fried. One thing I really miss is the American breakfast. I would have fried eggs done 'sunny side up' with 'hash browns' (fried potatoes). I would drink several cups of coffee and tuck into three large pancakes covered in maple syrup. After a breakfast like that I could walk a good 30 miles!

My walk along the Appalachian Trail was done as a training walk, in preparation for several major walks in the USA over the next few years. The trail proved to be a great experience. If you have five months' spare time, I couldn't think of a better way to enjoy the countryside, being in wilderness country, self—sufficient and learning a great deal about nature and about yourself. This quotation was carved on a board at Penmar —1,000 miles into the trail—and aptly describes my feelings.

> *"Remote for detachment, narrow for chosen company,*
> *winding for leisure, lonely for contemplation,*
> *the trail leads not only north and south, but*
> *upward to body, mind and soul of man."*

The organising body for the trail is the Appalachian Trail Conference, P.O. Box 807, Harpers Ferry, West Virginia, 25425, USA. They publish maps and guides to the trail. Ten guides cover the trail—North Carolina and Georgia; Tennessee and North Carolina; Central and Southern Virginia; Shenandoah National Park; Maryland and North Virginia; Pennsylvania; New York and New Jersey; Massachusetts and Connecticut; New Hampshire and Vermont; and Maine.

Suggested further reading—
From Katahdin to Springer Mountain—hiking stories Rodale Press 1977
The Appalachain Trail Ann and Myron Sutton Lippincott 1967
Appalachian Hiker II Edward B. Garvey Appalachian Books 1978
2000 Miles on the Appalachian Trail Donald J. Fortunato 1984
Walking With Spring—the first thru-hike Earl V. Shaffer ATC 1983
Ambling and Scrambling on the Appalachian Trail James M. & Hertha E. Flack ATC 1983
A Woman's Journey Cindy Ross East Woods Press 1982
The Appalachian Trail Ronald M. Fisher National Geographic Society 1972

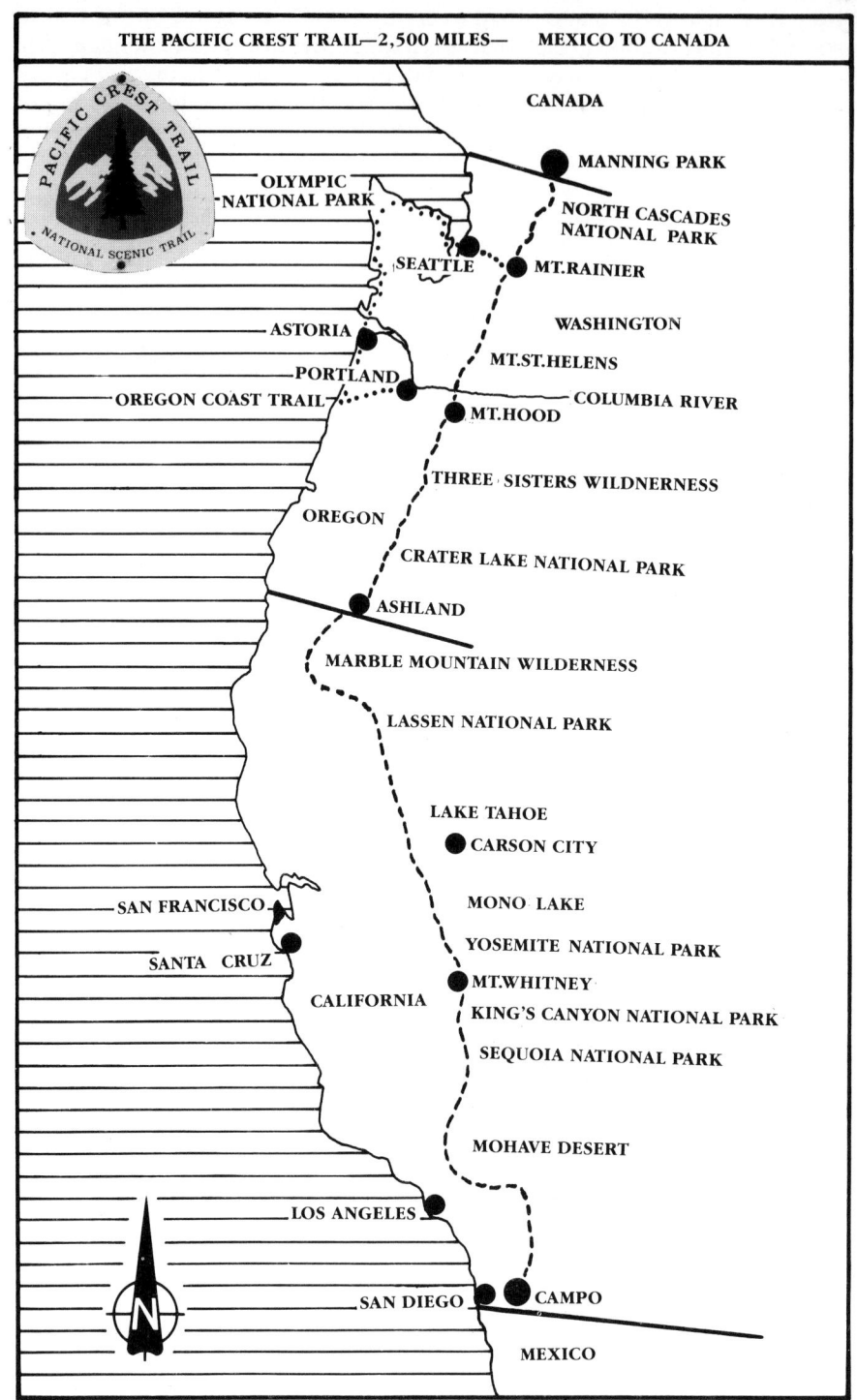

WALKWAY TO THE CLOUDS

It was in June 1971, while on a 900-mile walk through the Orkneys and Shetlands, that I first learnt about a 2,500-mile trail from Mexico to Canada. Known as the Pacific Crest Trail, the route was the idea of Clinton Clarke in the 1930s. Today it is the longest footpath in America, and their second National Scenic Trail. The arduous trail passes through all the climatic zones. On its journey through southern California the trail starts in deserts with temperatures up to 120°F. and ends up in 14,000 ft. mountains where the temperature barely reaches 40°F. The route includes some of the most scenic countryside in America—the High Sierras, Yosemite National Park, Lassen Volcanic Park, the volcanic mountains of Oregon—Mt. Jefferson and Mt. Hood—Mt. St. Helens in Washington and the Cascade mountains. It is truly a walkway to the clouds.

Following my walk around the coastline of Britain in 1978, I began my preparation for America. In April 1979 I set off from Springer Mountain in Georgia and walked the Appalachian Trail—2,200 miles—to Mt. Katahdin in Maine via fourteen states up the eastern side of America. I used this walk as an introduction to America and walking in remote wilderness areas. As part of my final preparation I did a walk in the European Alps and led a trek to Everest Base Camp! By early May 1980 my boots were broken in, equipment selected and tested, and my dehydrated food all parcelled up for posting to a dozen post offices along the route. My only item of equipment left was a tent, and this was made specially for me by Blacks of Greenock and arrived at the airport half an hour before I boarded the Los Angeles 'plane.

Following a 40-mile taxi ride from San Diego to the Mexican border at the small village of Campo, my hike northwards began. I signed in at the Post Office, and learnt that already 400 people had set off! Leaving my sixty-pound pack there, I walked to the border fence a mile away and photographed myself. Collecting my load I started, wondering how it would work out.

The first 700 miles of the route were largely through desert countryside to the High Sierra mountains. One day I would be walking along in temperatures well into the 90osF. as I crossed deserts, chaparral country and blowing sagebrush. The following day I would probably be toiling up a 9,000 foot mountain and camping in the snow. These first few weeks got my muscles hardened, saw me slowly getting fitter and used to carrying a heavy load. Four days out on the walk Mount St. Helens in Washington State blew up, but it would be a couple of months before I learnt the significance of this to the walk. In the deserts it was fascinating to see creatures almost like science—fiction, such as horned toads with their thick, scaly bodies, or iguanas on the rocks soaking up the heat. In a few places I would come across a hot spring and could strip and lie for half an hour soaking in nature's bath, while a can of food cooked in another pool close by.

I have never liked snakes, and on the Appalachian Trail I saw two of the most poisonous snakes in America, the rattlesnake and the copperhead. At first I jumped with alarm, but have now become used to seeing them. However, as I crossed the Mojave Desert I found a couple of Mojave Greens, the most poisonous snake in the whole of the Americas. One bite and you have only minutes to live. Unlike the Americans, I did not carry a snake-bite kit. The thought of cutting myself and using the suction cup did not appeal. Thankfully I was never bitten.

After 700 miles I reached Weldon in early June and collected my food parcel, containing 14 days' food, from the Post Office. The question now was what to do next. In the mountains so far I had encountered a lot of snow, and on Mount Baden Powell, for instance, had spent seven hours wading through snow to cover seven miles. All the reports I was getting advised not to cross the High Sierras, for they were covered with 200% more snow than normal. Never having been 'stopped' before on a major walk, I set off to see what it was like. I covered sixty miles before leaving the mountains. The snow was impossible to get through, but the main trouble was the rivers. I had already crossed some—there are no bridges—but they were bursting with snow-melt water, and it was folly to try and cross. After following one for ten miles trying to find a safe way to cross, I descended to the Owens Valley.

The valley is the alternative route, for it is not often that conditions allow you to walk the entire route without taking an alternative. The valley is the world's deepest, with 14,000 foot mountains on the west side and 12,000 foot mountains on the east. The walk up the valley is, therefore, very spectacular, especially with the mountains swamped in snow. The only unpleasant part was that I had to road-walk up Highway 395, a four-laned highway. It was the worst road I have ever undertaken. The road stretches in front of you for mile after mile. I followed it for 150 miles. Soon after setting off I saw Mt. Whitney, the highest mountain in the continental U.S.A. at 14,496 ft. I had planned to climb it, but now it was out of the question.

For the next two weeks I did a lot of road walking, but where possible I followed trails through the mountains, still encountering a lot of snow. It wasn't until northern California that I could pick up the trail proper. By now it was early July, and after more than sixty days of walking I had had no rain, only hot sun with temperatures rarely falling below 70°F. during the day. I wore a shirt and shorts, and looked disgustingly fit and bronzed! I had to detour into Yosemite to collect a food parcel, and spent a magnificent day walking high up around the valley. The sights of Half Dome and El Capitan brought tears to my eyes. To me it is the finest valley in the world; the beauty is breathtaking, especially as the waterfalls were at their best, being full of melt-water.

Half Dome — Yosemite National Park.

In northern California I walked through Lassen Volcanic National Park, my first introduction to the work of volcanoes. I crossed several lava flows, saw boiling lakes, geysers, boiling mud and ascended a cinder cone that erupted in 1851. Nothing grows in this area despite the fact that more than a century has elapsed since the eruption. After 1,600 miles from the Mexican border I called into a cobbler's shop in Burney and had my boots re-heeled. They lasted me for the rest of the walk. From here I stepped into some of the most beautiful scenery in California as I crossed the Marble Mountain Wilderness area. Frequently I went for half a dozen days and saw no-one, only black bears. At first they were alarming to see crossing the trail in front of you, but in time I learnt to admire them. At night they could be a nuisance, for they often came round the tent seeking food. At one time I had three, which made me feel very uncomfortable. I learnt later that four people had been killed by bears.

I was now walking extremely well, averaging 30 miles a day. To reach the State of Oregon I walked 93 miles in 54 hours and reached Ashland. My feet swelled alarmingly, so I relaxed for two days and went to three Shakespeare plays in the open-air theatre. The 500-mile section in Oregon is largely along a trail 5,000 feet up, passing through very remote wilderness areas. The area is also heavily forested, and a lot of the trail is in the shade. The trail comes close to several very impressive volcanoes—the Three Sisters, Mt. Jefferson and Mt. Hood—all of which are around the 11,000 ft. mark. They are very attractive mountains, with the added quality of having glaciers hanging down from their sides. I wanted to climb Mt. Hood, but because of heavy rockfalls I called it off. I had met only eight people walking the trail, but since the High Sierras I had seen no-one during the last six weeks. It was, therefore, quite a shock to round a bend in the trail and meet someone walking south to California with his dog laden with food panniers!

Beyond Mount Hood I descended down Eagle Creek to the Columbia River at Cascade Lochs. The other side of the river is Washington State, and the trail crosses the river here via the Bridge of Gods. I had now walked 2,100 miles in 85 days, and had to leave the trail for the section ahead through Giffard Pinchot National Forest was closed due to Mount St. Helens' eruption. The area was greatly devastated, and all the water sources were heavily polluted. It was possible to continue up the trail to Canada from Mount Rainier, (14,470 ft.), and I planned to walk there via the Olympic Peninsula.

To get to Mount Rainier on foot was a problem, as America is very car-orientated. Despite its size, there are only 150,000 miles of trail, and we in Britain have 150,000 miles of public rights of way. I could not walk on freeways, and so I had to get a bus to the coast and walk the Oregon Coast Trail to Astoria and the Columbia River, a walk of sixty miles. I could not cross the bridge, and so had to hitch a lift across! Then I could continue walking to the Olympics. This was another scenic gem, with glaciated mountains and dripping rain forests.

Using two ferries I reached Seattle, and fifty more miles brought me to Mount Rainier. By taking this detour, because of Mt. St. Helens, I had added on an extra 200 miles. I also had my rucksack repaired—nothing serious, just some of the stitching wearing away. Mt. Rainier is the most heavily glaciated mountain in America, and before I headed northwards for the final 350 miles I made an attempt to climb the mountain. I camped at 10,000 feet at Camp Muir and set off at 1.30 a.m., but two hours later turned back because of heavy rockfalls; it was just too dangerous.

Those final 360 miles to Canada stand out as some of the finest walking I have ever done. The scenery was exceptional at every twist of the trail. I saw no-one as I wove my way through the mountains. The last 100 miles were through the North Cascades National Park, which was not formed until 1968. In the park are more than 300 glaciers and some 200 black bears. I saw several, and was always careful to bag my food and suspend it from a tree at least 10 feet above the ground. I met up with a group of climbers from the Seattle Mountaineers Club, and I joined them on a 1,000 ft. climb and an 8,500 ft. mountain named the Tower. It was a fitting end to the walk.

I left them next morning and began the last 63 miles to Canada. I didn't want the walk to end, but I pressed on in top gear and reached Canada in 36 hours. The actual American/Canadian border is at Monument 78, eight miles from the nearest road. I photographed myself beside it and left a note, and hurried on to reach the road at Manning Park. I reached the Lodge there and stayed the night, and had my first bath for two weeks. I reflected on what I had done. I had become the first person to walk the whole trail that year, and in 118 days to walk it all, and although several hundred people set off from Campo each year only a handful actually make it. It was now early September, but in the final few days of the walk I had resolved that before leaving America I must climb Mount Whitney. I flew down to Los Angeles and took a Greyhound bus to Lone Pine. Here I stocked up with five days' food and set off for Whitney Portal, where I camped at 8,500 feet. The next day I continued ascending, and camped at well over 12,000 feet. The following day the dawn heralded a cloudless sky, and I set off to climb the final 2,000 feet of rock and snow. I reached the summit by noon, wearing thermal underwear with a temperature of −6°F. The view was unforgettable. There were the High Sierras at my feet, and the Owens Valley that I had walked up in June. After an hour I hurried on down to the tent. The next day I pressed on down to Lone Pine—in 10,000 feet of descent in six hours I had come from below zero temperatures to 95°F. at Lone Pine.

I had now achieved what I had wanted to do—to walk the entire Pacific Crest Trail and to climb Mount Whitney. For me it had been a walk of a lifetime, and by far the best walk I had ever done. I headed back to Los Angeles and home. I had been away for five months, but I had grown very fond of America and her people.

The following organisation publishes data sheets and Newsletters on the trail—Camp Research, P.O. Box 1907, Santa Ana, California, 92702, USA.

The Wilderness Press, 2440 Bancroft Way, Berkeley, California, 94704, USA—publish guides to the trail—
The Pacific Crest Trail Vol.1—California
The Pacific Crest Trail Vol.2—Oregon and Washington
Guide to the John Muir Trail Thomas Winnett
High Sierra Hiking Guide No 5—Mt Whitney Thomas Winnett

Suggested further reading—
A Hiker's Guide to the Oregon Coast Trail D.Bucy & M.McCauley Oregon State Parks
Pacific Crest Trail Hike Planning Guide Edited by Chuck Long Signpost Publications 1976
The High Adventure of Eric Ryback Chronicle Books 1971
A Pacific Crest Odyssey David Green Wilderness Press 1979
The Pacific Crest Trail Ann and Myron Sutton Lippincott 1975
The Pacific Crest Trail William R. Gray National Geographic Society 1975

OTHER BOOKS BY JOHN N. MERRILL & PUBLISHED BY JNM PUBLICATIONS

DAY WALK GUIDES

PEAK DISTRICT: SHORT CIRCULAR WALKS Fifteen carefully selected walks—3 to 5 miles—starting from a car park. The walks cover the variety of the area—the gritstone edges, limestone dales, and peat moorland. All follow well defined paths; include a pub for lunch; and are suitable for all the family. 44 pages 16 maps 32 photographs ISBN 0 907496 16 4

PEAK DISTRICT TOWN WALKS Twelve short circular walks around the principal towns and villages of the Peak District. Including Castleton, Buxton, Hathersage, Eyam, Tissington and Ashbourne. Each walk has a detailed map and extensive historical notes complete with pictures. 60 pages 12 maps 96 photographs ISBN 0 907496 20 2

PEAK DISTRICT: LONG CIRCULAR WALKS Fifteen differing walks 12 to 18 miles long for the serious hiker. Many follow lesser used paths in the popular areas, giving a different perspective to familiar landmarks. 64 pages 16 maps 28 photographs ISBN 0 907496 17 2

WESTERN PEAKLAND—CIRCULAR WALKS The first book to cover this remarkably attractive side of the National Park—west of Buxton. The guide combines both long and short walks. 25 -3 to 11 mile long walks with extremely detailed maps to help you explore the area. 48 pages 23 maps 22 photographs ISBN 0 907496 15 6

12 SHORT CIRCULAR WALKS AROUND MATLOCK 12 walks of about 4 miles long into the Matlock area rich in history and folklore and make ideal family outings. Included is an 'alpine' walk, using Matlock Bath's cable car as part of the route. 52 pages 44 photographs 12 maps ISBN 0 907496 25 3

SHORT CIRCULAR WALKS IN THE DUKERIES More than 25 walks in the Nottinghamshire/Sherwood Forest area, past many of the historic buildings that make up the Dukeries area. ISBN 0 907496 29 6

DERBYSHIRE AND THE PEAK DISTRICT CANAL WALKS More than 20 walks both short and long along the canals in the area—Cromford, Erewash, Chesterfield, Derby, Trent, Peak Forest and Macclesfield canals. ISBN 0 907496 30 X

HIKE TO BE FIT: STROLLING WITH JOHN John Merrill's personal guide to walking in the countryside to keep fit and healthy. He describes what equipment to use, where to go, how to map read, use a compass and what to do about blisters! 36 pages 23 photos 2 sketches 3 charts ISBN 0 907496 19 9

CHALLENGE WALKS

JOHN MERRILL'S PEAK DISTRICT CHALLENGE WALK A 25 mile circular walk from Bakewell, across valleys and heights involving 3,700 feet of ascent. More than 2,000 people have already completed the walk. A badge and completion certificate is available to those who complete. 32 pages 18 photographs 9 maps ISBN 0 907496 18 0

JOHN MERRILL'S YORKSHIRE DALES CHALLENGE WALK A 23 mile circular walk from Kettlewell in the heart of the Dales. The route combines mountain, moorlands, limestone country and dale walking with 3,600 feet of ascent. A badge and certificate is available to those who complete the route. 32 pages 16 photographs 8 maps ISBN 0 907196 28 8

THE RIVER'S WAY A two day walk of 43 miles, down the length of the Peak District National Park. Inaugurated and created by John, the walk starts at Edale, the end of the Pennine Way, and ends at Ilam. Numerous hostels, campgrounds, B&B, and pubs lie on the route, as you follow the five main river systems of the Peak—Noe, Derwent, Wye, Dove, and Manifold. 52 pages 35 photographs 7 maps
ISBN 0 907496 08 3

PEAK DISTRICT: HIGH LEVEL ROUTE A hard 90 mile, weeks walk, around the Peak District, starting from Matlock. As the title implies the walk keeps to high ground while illustrating the dramatic landscape of the Peak District. The walk was inaugurated and created by John and is used by him for training for his major walks! 60 pages 31 photographs 13 maps
ISBN 0 907496 10 5

PEAK DISTRICT MARATHONS The first reference book to gather together all the major and classical long walks of the Peak District between 25 and 50 miles long. Many are challenge walks with badges and completion cards for those who complete. The longest walk—280 miles —inaugurated by John is around the entire Derbyshire boundary. Each walk has a general map, accommodation list, and details of what guides and maps are needed. 56 pages 20 photographs 20 maps
ISBN 0 907496 13 X

HISTORICAL GUIDES

WINSTER—A VISITOR'S GUIDE A detailed look at a former lead mining community which still retains a Morris dancing team and annual pancake races. A two mile walk brings you to many historical buildings including the 17th century Market House. Illustrated by old photographs. 20 pages 21 photographs 1 map
ISBN 0 907496 21 0

DERBYSHIRE INNS The first book to tell the story behind more than 150 inns in the Peak District and Derbyshire area. With details of legends, murders and historical anecdotes, the book gives added pleasure or impetus to explore the pubs of the region. Profusely illustrated with 65 photographs and a brief history of brewing in Derbyshire. 68 pages 57 photographs 5 maps
ISBN 0 907496 11 3

100 HALLS AND CASTLES OF THE PEAK DISTRICT AND DERBYSHIRE A visitor's guide to the principal historical buildings of the region. Many are open to the public and the guide describes the history of the building from the Domesday Book to the present time. The book is illustrated by 120 photographs and makes an excellent souvenir gift of one of England's finest architectural areas. 120 pages 116 photographs 4 maps
ISBN 0 907496 23 7

TOURING THE PEAK DISTRICT AND DERBYSHIRE Twenty circular routes of about 50 miles for the motorist or cyclist. Each route has a set theme, such as the gritstone edges or in the steps of Mary, Queen of Scots. Deatiled maps for each route and fifty photographs make this a useful companion to the Peak District/Derbyshire area. 76 pages 45 photographs 20 maps
ISBN 0 907496 22 9

JOHN'S MARATHON WALKS

EMERALD COAST WALK The story of John's walk up the total length of the west coast of Ireland and exploration of more than fifty islands—1,600 miles. 132 pages 32 photographs 12 maps
ISBN 0 907496 02 4

TURN RIGHT AT LAND'S END In 1978 John Merrill became the first person to walk the entire coastline of Britain—6,824 miles in ten months. The book details the route, how he ascended our three major mountains and how he found a wife. Included are more than 200 photographs he took on the walk, which is also a unique guide to our coastline. 246 pages 214 photographs 10 maps
ISBN 0 907496 24 5

WITH MUSTARD ON MY BACK John has gathered together the stories of his first decade of walking—1970-1980. Here is a collection of unique walks in Britain, from a 2,000 mile walk linking the ten National Parks of England and Wales together to a 450 mile walk from Norwich to Durham.
ISBN 0 907496 27 X

TURN RIGHT AT DEATH VALLEY During the summer of 1984, John walked coast to coast across America, a distance of 4,226 miles in 177 days. Few have walked across and none have taken so difficult a route. He crossed all the main mountain ranges, climbed 14,000 foot mountains, crossed deserts in 100 degrees, walked rim to rim of the Grand Canyon in 8 1/2 hours, and crossed the famed Death Valley. The walk is without parallel and the story is the remarkable tale of this unique adventure.
ISBN 0 907496 26 1